MW00366365

CINCINNATI MOMENTS

To the people of Cincinnati

Cover: *Suspension Bridge at dawn*
A towboat and its litter of barges
are wreathed in the river's wintry
breath as frigid air meets warmer
water on the second-coldest day in
Cincinnati's history. Temperatures
fell to 24.3 degrees below zero.

January 19, 1994

Glenn Hartong

Copyright © 2000 *The Cincinnati Enquirer*

All rights reserved.
No part of this book
may be used or reproduced
in any manner whatsoever
without written permission.

Library of Congress catalog
card number: 00-133412

ISBN 0-9630442-3-0

Designed by Grannan Graphic Design

Printed in Cincinnati, Ohio
The Merten Company

Revised and Expanded

CINCINNATI
MOMENTS

A celebration of photographs from
THE CINCINNATI ENQUIRER

Written by Cliff Radel

Edited by Sue Lancaster
Photos edited by Liz Dufour

FOREWORD

Welcome to the Big Red Machine edition of *Cincinnati Moments*. This is our home. So we take a special pride in bringing the news of our region to our neighbors each day.

We feel the same way about *Cincinnati Moments*, a collection of memorable moments in time.

Since April 10, 1841, *The Enquirer* has delivered the news from around the Tristate, the nation, the world – even outer space – to Greater Cincinnati.

In all that time, 159 years, there have been millions of moments. Most were good. Some, however, brought news that was tragic beyond belief.

The following pages reflect many of those moments, good and bad, captured in words and photographs from *The Cincinnati Enquirer*.

The first edition of *Cincinnati Moments,* released in November 1999, sold out in a month. This revised edition includes even more up-to-date photos as well as a chapter devoted to the 1975 and 1976 World Champion Cincinnati Reds – the Big Red Machine.

The new *Cincinnati Moments* comes at an opportune time. As a new century and a new millennium unfold, the world is rushing into the future.

Before we get too caught up in the coming attractions, though, we should take a moment to look over our shoulders and reflect on the past. Remember, for instance, the Reds' glory years.

We need a clear picture of where we have been to know where we are going.

The stories and photos in *Cincinnati Moments* provide directions for this journey. Enjoy the ride.

Harry W Whipple

Harry M. Whipple
President and Publisher
The Cincinnati Enquirer

Ward H. Bushee

Ward H. Bushee
Editor/Vice President
The Cincinnati Enquirer

CONTENTS

Looking north at Fifth and Vine, the former Enquirer Building in the distance.

February 1927

Walter B. Oelze

INTRODUCTION	6
CHAPTER 1 The Genius of Water	8
CHAPTER 2 Through the Looking Glass	28
CHAPTER 3 This Is the News	66
CHAPTER 4 City of Champions	106
CHAPTER 5 "And This One Belongs to the Reds"	142
BIOGRAPHIES	178
ACKNOWLEDGMENTS	179
INDEX	180

FLOOD AID
January 31, 1937

Lawrence J. Neumann

INTRODUCTION

I come from a long line of tour guides. My grandparents had the job first, showing off Cincinnati to visiting relatives. Then they turned it over to my mom and dad. Now, it's my turn with *Cincinnati Moments, a Celebration of Photographs from The Cincinnati Enquirer.*

Like my parents' tours, this book visits the area's high and low spots. It points out what makes the city tick and the kinds of people who live here. This Big Red Machine edition also devotes a chapter to Sparky Anderson's Reds, the back-to-back 1975 and 1976 World Championship teams of Pete Rose, Johnny Bench, Joe Morgan and Tony Perez.

Selected from thousands of worthy candidates, the photos and stories in this revised and expanded *Cincinnati Moments* make you feel welcome. They issue an invitation to stay a while, get to know the town, meet its people, root for the home team. Recalling good times and bad, *Cincinnati Moments* chronicles life in a place that treasures small-town values as it pursues big-city dreams.

The photos, culled from the archives of *The Enquirer,* offer a mix of portraits and still lifes, landscapes and cityscapes, dreamy shots and an occasional nightmarish image from the news. They span 97 years, from 1904 to 2000. Each decade of the 20th century, as well as several new millennium moments, is represented.

Cincinnati Moments is a team effort. Ron Huff, Sue Lancaster, Alan Vonderhaar and I selected the photos for the Big Red Machine edition. Ron designed the pages, while Alan employed his computer wizardry to enhance both aging prints and modern digital images. For the book's first edition, Liz Dufour compiled the photographs and Michael E. Keating handled the restoration work. For both editions, my wife, Debbie, conducted countless historical investigations as I researched and wrote the stories behind the photos. Sue Lancaster edited the book and kept us in line and on time. Marti Flanagan watched over us so we stayed true to our mission.

To qualify for *Cincinnati Moments,* a photograph had to be more than a pretty picture. Each photo, whether it came from near or far, had to capture an event, a face, a place or a slice of everyday life that says Cincinnati.

Many early photos failed to make the cut, including *The Enquirer's* first news photographs. These mugshots, featuring the stern faces of Civil War veterans, appeared on September 5, 1898, 57 years after *The Enquirer* debuted.

From 1898 until the 1920s, when the newspaper started hiring full-time photographers, most photos in *The Enquirer* depicted either faces or places, dignitaries' portraits or houses where crimes were committed. Photographs from these years are scarce in *Cincinnati Moments.*

Until the 1940s, the vast majority of *Enquirer* photos appeared in the newspaper without identifying who took the picture. So, many early images in this book are attributed to: Photographer unknown. Credited or not, the photos can be enjoyed for their immediacy and the glimpses they provide into years gone by, be it kids saluting a passing flag or victims reacting to the cruelty of a tornado.

Through words and pictures, this collection of moments shows just how deeply rooted Cincinnati remains in its traditions. The city is still linked to the river. The Ohio can be Cincinnati's best friend or its worst enemy.

The people of Cincinnati balance an Old-World reserve with a generous spirit. They can be thin-skinned and warm-hearted, tight-lipped and fun-loving – all at the same time.

The following pages offer both a panoramic view and a personality profile of this river city, from the hills to the valley below, from the tragedies its people have endured to the laughter they've shared.

All make up *Cincinnati Moments*.

– **Cliff Radel**

CITY IN A MIST
October 7, 1986

Ed Reinke

Streams of water and beams of light spin
a misty web around the symbol of Cincinnati.
This 19th-century gift from hardware merchant
Henry Probasco "To the People of Cincinnati"
honored his late brother-in-law and civic-minded
business partner, Tyler Davidson. Dedicated on
October 6, 1871, the Tyler Davidson Fountain
is the heart of this river city. When sweet dreams
come true, when a war ends, when the Reds win
a World Series, when lovers share their first kiss,
"the people of Cincinnati" celebrate in front
of the fountain topped by a nine-foot-tall
bronze lady named "The Genius of Water."

CHAPTER 1

THE GENIUS OF WATER

TYLER DAVIDSON FOUNTAIN
July 16, 1953

Herb Heise

9

Giant fingers of ice dwarf payroll clerk Delores Haynes as she trudges past the Wareham Drive retaining wall in Mount Adams. This wasn't the worst of it, though. Two weeks after this photo appeared in *The Enquirer*, the Blizzard of 1978 shut down the city. People able to dig out their newspapers the next morning read that five inches of new snow had landed on a one-inch-thick layer of ice and five inches of old snow. Falling temperatures and 49-mph winds created whiteout conditions and a windchill factor of 52 degrees below zero. The weather outside was so frightful, not even the mail could get through.

MOUNT ADAMS
January 11, 1978

Alex Burrows

10

Summers like to sneak up on Cincinnati. While spring
lingers – it's often too cold and rainy or too warm
and rainy – summer just appears. Overnight, the weather
goes from barely bearable to totally unbearable. The sun
blazes. The humidity soars. When that happens, nothing
cools down a kid quite like a romp under a sprinkler.
Water cascades over Yohna Israel's bare chest, chasing away
the heat, bringing on a smile of relief, drop by cooling drop.

SUMMER SPRINKLER
June 25, 1987

Michael E. Keating

11

Anyone up for a brisk stroll could walk the Ohio River in 1904
and again in 1977. During those years, the winter weather was so cold,
for such a long time, the river froze.

The Ohio wasn't rock solid from surface to riverbed. But the freeze
was long enough – 56 days during the winter of 1903-04 – and thick
enough – 12 inches on January 19, 1977 – for daredevils to walk
from Cincinnati to Covington. And back.

In 1904, river walkers passed the packet boat *Bonanza*, locked in
a 37-mile-long ice jam. They stepped gingerly over cakes of ice,
similar to those encountered by Eliza during her river crossing in
Uncle Tom's Cabin.

In 1977, kids in jeans and sneakers stepped lively upon reaching
the midpoint of their trek from Kentucky to Ohio. Few paused
in the middle of the river. Out there, the ice was at its thinnest,
creaking and groaning as the current below flowed toward New Orleans.

FROZEN OHIO RIVER
February 1904

Helen Drahman

RIVER WALKERS
January 19, 1977

Bob Lynn

13

From a distance, this saltscape at Cincinnati's highway maintenance facility in Camp Washington could be mistaken for a sandy beach on a tropical island – far, far away from the frostbitten city, where winter paves the hilly streets with ice and snow. During the winter of 1999-2000, Cincinnati used 17,000 tons of the granulated melting agent. That's four tons of slush-producing salt for every street, lane, avenue and boulevard in town.

ROAD SALT
November 2, 1977

Ed Reinke

A slice of frosted gingerbread from 1904, Eden Park's gazebo stands empty as a couple forsakes its promise of shelter to trudge through the aftermath of a late-winter storm.

Light dustings are greeted warmly in Cincinnati. Such weather seldom sticks around, turning quickly from snowflakes to snowmen to slush.

But when a dusting turns to "measurable accumulation," as the TV forecasters say, the snow rapidly wears out its welcome. Temperatures can plummet, frigid winds howl and cars slide around corners.

Cincinnatians are skittish about snow. The mere mention of it in the forecast sends drivers into a panic. Road crews coat the asphalt with salt, and shoppers clear the stores of the four staples of a storm: milk, bread, toilet paper and beer.

EDEN PARK
March 9, 1999

Tony Jones

At 14 degrees below zero, the Ohio River steams and Paul Goff shivers. The deckhand aboard the Anderson Ferry boat has a bitterly cold job. Although the morning sun's rays have applied a layer of gold leaf to the wintry landscape, the safety cables Goff struggles to adjust are as cold and unforgiving as a pile of steel beams. Ferrymen and their boats have been battling winters at this spot on the Ohio since 1817. Linking western Hamilton County to Constance on the Kentucky shore, the Anderson Ferry has survived the Civil War, railroads, interstates, tornadoes and floods, as well as freezes so deep even the river's breath turned to ice.

ANDERSON FERRY
December 21, 1989

Glenn Hartong

Mother and child look on anxiously as
Dr. Byron Nellans, dean of the Eclectic Medical
College, examines a squirming patient.
Nurse Lois Hunterman, from Bethesda Hospital,
cradles the boy's head. All in a day's work at
Guilford School during the Flood of 1937.
The downtown school became a Red Cross shelter
for East End families left homeless by the
rising waters.

The flood reached its peak the day of this exam.
The Ohio River crested – after claiming eight
lives and causing an estimated $65 million in
damage – at 79.9 feet, a record that still stands
in Cincinnati.

20

The 1937 flood, Cincinnati's worst
natural disaster, turned downtown streets
into a latticework of canals. This is no flotilla
of gondolas in search of passengers. The river
is receding, and the Coast Guard boats bobbing
in the swirling waters are preparing to shove off
for Louisville, Kentucky, another river town
devastated by the flood's wrath.

Three days earlier, the flood did its best
to drown Cincinnati. Fed by two inches of rain
and six inches of melting snow, the rising waters
closed the waterworks. Much of the city was
without electricity. Along the Ohio River, fuel
tanks spilled their contents into the water and the
river caught fire. Small wonder that January 24,
1937, came to be known as "Black Sunday."

**FLOOD OF '37
THIRD AND VINE**
January 27, 1937

Photographer unknown

Trucks, cars and pedestrians line up to cross the Suspension Bridge. The span has just opened to regular traffic for the first time since the 1937 flood swamped Greater Cincinnati.

Its approaches sandbagged and its roadbed just above the river's record crest of 79.9 feet, the bridge allowed emergency crossings throughout the disaster. Seventy years old in 1937, the landmark link between Ohio and Kentucky was the only bridge to remain open during the flood along 800 miles of river from Steubenville, Ohio to Cairo, Illinois.

At the time this photo was taken, workers in the foreground were being issued brooms and shovels to remove flood debris. The Hostess Cake truck waiting to cross the bridge signaled that life in the beleaguered cities along the Ohio finally was returning to normal.

FLOOD OF '37
COVINGTON, KENTUCKY
January 29, 1937

Photographer unknown

23

FLOOD OF '48
April 17, 1948

Ran Cochran

Two floods, same river, different eras. One photo looking down from a tower of the Suspension Bridge. The other from a helicopter.

Many nasty floods have done their best to wash over this bend in the river, including the floods of 1948 and 1997. They stand, respectively, as the eighth- and ninth-highest floods in the history of Cincinnati.

In 1948, Cincinnatians went down to the Ohio primarily to work, loading and unloading barges, piloting ferries, toiling in riverfront factories, warehouses and scrap heaps.

By 1997, the river and the riverfront had become Cincinnati's playground. Pleasure boats zipped up and down the Ohio. Drab riverfront workplaces gave way to a stadium, an arena, the Serpentine Wall and Bicentennial Commons.

Whether the Ohio is a place to work or to play, nothing is safe when its storm-fed waters overflow their banks.

The floods of 1948 and 1997 trashed whatever they touched. The currents smashed buildings, submerged the landscape and separated us from the things we hold dear.

The floods humbled us. They reminded everyone that it's all right to build by the Ohio and have fun in its waters.

Just remember: The river is still the boss.

FLOOD OF '97
March 4, 1997

Ernest Coleman

The *Delta Queen* steams into the dawn along the Ohio's still waters. Bound for her home port of Cincinnati, she last stopped in Louisville, where the sternwheeler joined in a week of hullabaloo over the Kentucky Derby.

Prowling America's inland waterways since 1927, she is the last of her kind, a steam-powered paddle-wheeler with a wooden superstructure, carrying passengers on overnight cruises. On the National Register of Historic Places and recognized as a National Historic Landmark, the vessel recalls a graceful era when steamboats with tall, black smokestacks and red paddle wheels dotted the river and Cincinnati reigned as the "Queen City of the West."

THE *DELTA QUEEN*
May 5, 1981

Michael E. Keating

CHAPTER 2

THROUGH THE LOOKING GLASS

These were serious times. America was at war, fighting a losing battle on two fronts. Four months after attacking Pearl Harbor, the Japanese controlled the Pacific and a good chunk of Asia. In Europe, most of the continent belonged to Hitler.

Back home, round-faced little boys put on soldier suits and sailor hats and went to parades for the men and women marching off to war.

From Hamilton County alone, 1,855 never returned.

**ARMY DAY PARADE
DOWNTOWN**
April 7, 1942

Robert E. Stigers

Stealing one last kiss before the troop train pulls away from Norwood's B&O station, Ruth Lindeman clings to the arms of her husband-to-be, Jack Driscoll. He's on his way to Wisconsin for three weeks of summer maneuvers with the Ohio National Guard. She plans to wait for him to come home to Norwood. They are getting married in September 1940. Over the next five years, this scene would be repeated time and again – 92,000 troops from Cincinnati received similar goodbye kisses before heading off to World War II.

B&O STATION
NORWOOD
August 11, 1940

Photographer unknown

Despite losing his leg on a warship,
William N. Morton proudly marches on the
30th anniversary of the end of World War I.

In 1954, Congress changed the name of the
holiday to Veterans Day – a day to honor
all veterans.

Like the pavers and the rails on Main Street,
Cincinnati's Veterans Day parades are also
a thing of the past. The cost of insurance and
cleanup put an end to the parades in which
William N. Morton once marched on two crutches
and one leg.

ARMISTICE DAY PARADE
MAIN AND COURT STREETS
November 11, 1948

Carl Wellinger

"Wanna-bag-o'-peanuts?"

He would sing out his question as one word, salted with a South Carolina accent.

Peanut Jim Shelton sold peanuts for 50 years from pushcarts he called "Cadillacs." Plying his trade with great dignity, he became one of the city's finest ambassadors. He roasted his peanuts by hand and hawked them all over town: on the Suspension Bridge at rush hour, from his Liberty Street shop in Over-the-Rhine, and at Crosley Field when the Reds were in town.

When the Reds moved to Riverfront Stadium in 1970, Peanut Jim moved with them.

In 1971, the ballclub claimed his sales were hurting the Reds' concession business. Reds management tried to keep him from parking his Cadillac cart on a walkway leading to the stadium.

But Peanut Jim prevailed. He sold peanuts on that walkway until a few days before his death at age 93 in 1982. Three years later, the city named that walkway in his honor.

PEANUT JIM
February 26, 1973

Gerry Wolter

32

Her trademark corsage pinned to a lapel or tied to her microphone, Ruth Lyons held sway, first on radio, then on TV, from 1931 until she retired in 1967. Her *50-50 Club*, an unscripted talk show with music and world-famous guests, was the most powerful program in the Tristate.

Ruth Lyons grew up poor in the East End. She admitted she didn't have a face for television or a voice for radio, but her honest gift of gab earned a loyal following and astronomically high ratings.

Ruth Lyons died in 1988. But her name and goodwill live on with the Ruth Lyons Children's Fund, which she began in 1939 to buy toys for hospitalized children. Since then, it has raised nearly $21 million.

RUTH LYONS
June 1948

Carl Wellinger

Five cousins get cozy on a Fifth Street curb as Mai-Tai,
a Cincinnati Zoo elephant, lumbers by adorned in shamrocks.
Members of the Ancient Order of Hibernians established
the annual St. Patrick's Day Parade in 1967 to honor Ireland's
patron saint as well as the Irish who came to Cincinnati
in the 19th century. Fleeing the famines of the 1840s
and 1850s, the immigrants landed at the present-day site of
Bicentennial Commons before heading for neighborhoods to the
north and west. The Irish made many contributions to the city's
history, including a floating soap. James Gamble,
Procter & Gamble's co-founder, came from northern Irish stock.

ST. PATRICK'S DAY PARADE
DOWNTOWN
March 16, 1980

Dick Swaim

The *Majestic* prepares to dock at Cincinnati's Public Landing during Tall Stacks '95.

Tall, flared smokestacks vent vapors toward the sky. Cherry-red paddle wheels churn the water. And steam calliopes hiss out tunes as the huge, flat-bottomed boats, their wide white decks stacked like layers of a wedding cake, float past the crowds.

Spun off Cincinnati's bicentennial celebration in 1988 and repeated in 1992, 1995 and 1999, Tall Stacks encourages the city to kick off those conservative wingtips and slip into some dancing shoes . . . to relive the days when the "Queen City of the West" was a bold, rowdy town on a river teeming with temptation.

TALL STACKS '95
OHIO RIVER
October 11, 1995

Glenn Hartong

Samantha cuddles her baby daughter, Jackie,
at the Cincinnati Zoo's Gorilla World. The exhibit
holds the U.S. record for having the most gorillas
who like to monkey around. As of 2000, 47 gorillas
were born there. Only London's Howletts Zoo had
more, with 63. Samantha has done her part. She
was born at the zoo. So were her five daughters and
one son. And of the 47 Cincinnati-born gorillas,
10 call Samantha "Grandma."

CINCINNATI ZOO
June 6, 1990

Jim Callaway

Swimming in success, silver and red-belly pacu attend a dinner party with a red-tailed catfish at the Newport Aquarium. Diver Kay Kinsey serves them a meal of smelt, shrimp and herring.

In its first year of operation, the aquarium on the Ohio River's southern shore greeted 1,251,292 visitors, 50,000 above the wildest projection.

The 1-million-gallon aquarium and another new tourist attraction, the 33-ton bronze World Peace Bell, symbolize Newport's remarkable transformation. The Northern Kentucky town once reigned as the area's "Sin City." Now, it thrives on good, clean fun.

NEWPORT AQUARIUM
May 12, 2000

Patrick Reddy

WORLD PEACE BELL
August 1, 1999

Craig Ruttle

Pearls of beer suds float to earth as a dirndl-clad
Kay Beiderbeck wins the Gemütlichkeit
"Sprint for the Stein" race, a prelude to the
annual Oktoberfest-Zinzinnati – a celebration
of the city's considerable German heritage.

The two-day Oktoberfest pulls 500,000 people
downtown to eat German food and drink beer.

Cincinnatians once had an unquenchable thirst
for the hoppy, foamy stuff. In 1893, the city
had 35 breweries and produced 1.3 million barrels
of beer a year. The annual per-capita consumption
of the hometown brews measured 50 gallons.

**OKTOBERFEST-ZINZINNATI
FOUNTAIN SQUARE**
September 14, 1984

Ed Reinke

Clean at last, Cincinnati's symbol radiates a warm bronze glow. Abused by years of neglect, the Tyler Davidson Fountain underwent a much-needed restoration in 2000.

To remove layers of green gunk, grime and corrosion, foundry worker Justin Summersell sprays a pressurized mixture of water and powdered glass on one of four drinking fountains ringing the base of the city's most famous work of art.

A 1998 inspection found the fountain in grave condition. The Genius of Water, the lady atop the fountain, listed to one side. The foundation was crumbling. Left untouched, the landmark would collapse.

News of the fountain's plight launched a successful campaign to raise $3 million in private funds – $2 million for restoration, and $1 million for a maintenance endowment to make sure the city's symbol would never fall into disrepair again.

TYLER DAVIDSON FOUNTAIN
FOUNTAIN SQUARE
March 9, 2000

Glenn Hartong

41

CINCINNATI RIVERFRONT
July 14, 2000

Glenn Hartong

Shedding light on the rebirth of Cincinnati's riverfront, Paul Brown Stadium glows along the skyline. The first test of the stadium's lights took place as the very last rays of day turned the Ohio River into a velvet ribbon of violet.

The Bengals' new 65,600-seat facility opened August 19, 2000, signaling a renaissance of the Ohio's northern shore.

Upriver, the Reds' Great American Ball Park will replace Cinergy Field. The space between the stadiums is to be filled by a park and The Banks complex of shops, housing and restaurants.

Anchoring it all will be a shrine to freedom: the National Underground Railroad Freedom Center.

FIRST GAME
PAUL BROWN STADIUM
August 19, 2000

Glenn Hartong

43

Faithful pilgrims continue the Good Friday tradition of saying a prayer on each step as they climb the stairs to the Church of the Immaculate Conception high atop Mount Adams.

The rite began in 1861, a year after the church, now known as Holy Cross-Immaculata Church, was dedicated. Depending on the size of the crowd and the duration of the prayers, it takes about 90 minutes to climb the 356 steps from Columbia Parkway. Some pilgrims feel, when they reach the last step, that they have scaled Mount Adams. Others believe they are 356 steps closer to heaven.

GOOD FRIDAY
MOUNT ADAMS
April 12, 1963

Fred Straub

Sunlight playing on her gossamer veil, a woman
climbs the stairs inside the Islamic Center
of Greater Cincinnati. An unseen stained-glass
window in the West Chester house of worship
scatters rays of an early-morning sun, painting
a rainbow of colors on a nearby wall. Beneath
the woman, men bow their heads in prayer.

At the center, men and women worship apart.
Men on the first floor. Women in the balcony.
Their prayers mark the first day of Eid al-Fitr.
The Feast of Breaking Fast comes at the end of
Ramadan, the most holy month for Muslims.

EID al-FITR
WEST CHESTER
January 29, 1998

Steven M. Herppich

DWARF IRIS
EDEN PARK
March 2, 1998

Glenn Hartong

Winter coats clash with Easter bonnets in a line of visitors inching toward Eden Park's Krohn Conservatory. Despite occasional snow flurries, the crowd waits patiently to see the spring floral display.

The conservatory's opening in 1933 helped Cincinnatians establish this Easter ritual: Dress up. Attend church. Visit the Krohn. Marvel at the lilies. Sniff the orchids. See the cacao tree, supplier of candy eggs' main ingredient. Toss pennies for good luck into the fish pond next to the banana tree.

Easter Sunday remains Krohn's busiest day of the year. The parking lot fills before the doors open at 7 a.m.

Easter's message of rebirth blooms outside the conservatory, as well. A pair of dwarf iris – sometimes called fleur-de-lis, or "flower of the lily" – present their blossoms of blue amid tender shoots and tufts of evergreens, fulfilling spring's eternal promise of life everlasting.

EASTER SUNDAY
KROHN CONSERVATORY
March 25, 1951

Herb Heise

On the day after Thanksgiving, even the metal railing rimming the sidewalk at Fifth and Vine can't restrain the bargain hunters outside the Mabley & Carew department store. Before suburban malls, this is how downtown Cincinnati looked at the opening of the holiday shopping season.

People made a day of it.

They window-shopped and admired the decorations. After lunch, there was a Graeter's sundae. Later in the afternoon, a shopper's stamina was restored by a bag of soft pretzels. During the holidays, a burly man bundled in a huge woolen overcoat sold the pretzels from a wicker basket outside Shillito's department store. And no trip downtown on the day after Thanksgiving would be complete without walking over to the CG&E building to stare in wonder at the model trains.

HOLIDAY SHOPPERS DOWNTOWN
November 29, 1946

Carl Wellinger

Tony Bennett never would have left his heart in San Francisco if Cincinnati still had the Mount Adams Incline.

Streetcars climbed halfway to the stars as the incline gently pulled them 975.6 feet from the base of Mount Adams to the summit on Celestial Street. The journey aboard a platform on an inclined plane took 2½ minutes.

For 72 years, ample numbers of tourists and locals alike went up the hill to see the sights. The last streetcar made the grade on July 25, 1947. Even after buses replaced the streetcars, the Mount Adams Incline averaged 5,000 weekday passengers, 8,000 on Sundays. Some walked to the Cincinnati Art Museum and Rookwood Pottery. Others took in the view of the Ohio River Valley, Cincinnati's skyline and the hills of Kentucky.

Closed in 1948 because its owners did not want to spend $126,000 on repairs, the incline was the last of Cincinnati's hill-climbing railways. Inclines also traveled up Mount Auburn and Price Hill, as well as the hills of Clifton and Fairview. But none lasted as long or offered a better view than the incline to Mount Adams.

MOUNT ADAMS INCLINE
Fall 1946

Allan Kain

Millions of dollars of taxpayers' money went into Cincinnati's subway system. All the city had to show for it was this hole in the ground. The hole eventually was covered up. But not before two miles of underground tunnels were built, along with seven miles of platforms and passageways. Cincinnati's subway had strong public support. In 1916, voters approved a $6.1 million rapid-transit bond issue by a ratio of six to one. Construction started in 1920 along what is now Central Parkway. The subway system was abandoned after funds ran out or disappeared (depending on which account you believe) in 1927. The bonds were finally paid off in 1966. With interest, the final tally was $13 million.

BUILDING THE SUBWAY
CENTRAL PARKWAY
October 1920

Photographer unknown

Idled by a threatened rail strike, passenger cars fill a maze of tracks in the West End.

Taken at dusk from the Western Hills Viaduct, this panoramic photo shows the dome of Union Terminal's rotunda looking toward the light stanchions of Crosley Field.

If the strike had gone into effect, 1,000 workers would have been laid off at the terminal. And the Reds, ending a homestand at Crosley Field, would have been forced to fly to their next game against the Cubs instead of taking a train to Chicago.

But the strike never materialized.

And the baseball team did not have to change its travel plans.

The same day this photo was taken, President Harry Truman seized the railroads to avert "a nationwide tragedy."

The strike was off. The trains rolled on.

52

**RAILYARD
WEST END**
May 10, 1948

Allan Kain

CONEY ISLAND
May 1928

Harry Pence

Sporting straw hats, suits and dresses, fun-seekers stroll the mall at Coney Island. Roller-coaster cars climb distant tracks as the Ferris wheel pauses between rides. Many of these visitors came to the park aboard the *Island Queen*. At a length of 285 feet, the *Queen* held 4,100 passengers on five decks painted bright white and lit up at night by the glow of 7,000 light bulbs. Passengers could dance across the wooden floor in the two-story ballroom or go to the top deck for romance as the *Queen* took her time paddling up and down the river. The steamboat served the park from 1926 until September 9, 1947, when a spark from a welding torch started a fire while the boat was docked in Pittsburgh.

Within seconds, the paddle-wheeler exploded, ending a 66-year tradition of steamboats ferrying passengers between Cincinnati's Public Landing and the amusement park.

After the *Queen* exploded, Coney Island expanded its parking lots until it ran out of room. Coney's owners then went north to build Kings Island. The original Coney closed in 1971, 24 years after the *Island Queen* was lost to a spark.

One modest parking lot, railroad tracks and a baseball diamond in the distance compete for space on the front lawn of Ivorydale, flagship factory of Procter & Gamble.

In 1927, P&G had four American plants and sales of $162 million. The company was making floating bars of Ivory (introduced in 1879) and Crisco shortening (1911). Ivorydale was gearing up to sell a new perfumed soap with a cameo on the wrapper, called Camay.

By 2000, the company did business in 140 countries, producing 300 brands of soaps, toothpaste, cleaning products, cosmetics, cooking oils, fat-free potato chips and paper goods.

P&G started in Cincinnati on October 31, 1837. Two brothers-in-law, candlemaker William Procter and soap-maker James Gamble, each chipped in $3,596.47 – one of the best investments ever. By 2000, annual sales were almost $40 billion.

PROCTER & GAMBLE
IVORYDALE, ST. BERNARD
Summer 1927

Photographer unknown

Propeller-driven passenger planes await
instructions from the control tower atop the
terminal building at Greater Cincinnati Airport.

In its seven years of existence, the 900-acre
airport had already tripled its passenger count,
from 300,000 in 1947 to 912,396 in 1954.

Today, that dinky building is Terminal 1.
It houses three airlines and the airport's
administrative offices.

Now known as the Cincinnati/Northern
Kentucky International Airport, the facility has
grown to 7,000 acres and serves nearly
23 million passengers a year.

GREATER CINCINNATI AIRPORT
BOONE COUNTY, KENTUCKY
1954

Bob Free

58

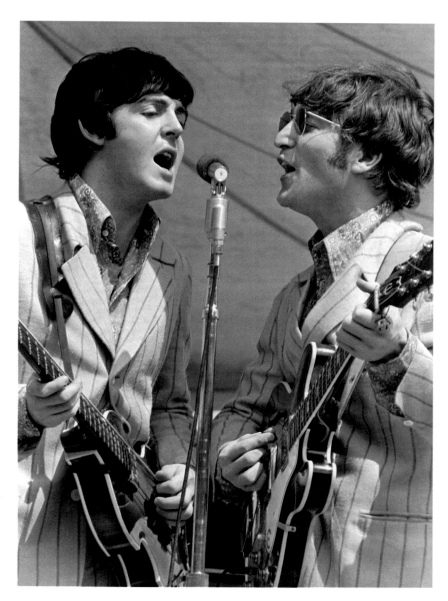

The Beatles visited Cincinnati during the dog days of August in 1964 and 1966 – despite a February 22, 1964, editorial in *The Cincinnati Enquirer* branding them "the greatest divisive influence in the United States since the issue of slavery."

The most expensive ticket for both concerts was $5.50. Neither of the Fab Four's shows lasted longer than 30 minutes. At the Gardens, the sold-out crowd numbered 14,000. Scads of fans stood on their chairs for a better view as the Beatles began their show with "Twist and Shout."

Two years later, 30,000 tickets were available for the Crosley Field stop on what turned out to be the Beatles' final American tour. After rain washed out a Saturday show, the Beatles performed on Sunday for a crowd of 22,500. After the Beatles took the stage, Paul McCartney and John Lennon shared a microphone and the crowd screamed. The cheering continued even after the Beatles had hopped off the stage and vanished through an open gate in center field.

LENNON AND McCARTNEY
CROSLEY FIELD
August 21, 1966

Fred Straub

BEATLES FANS
CINCINNATI GARDENS
August 27, 1964

Bob Free

Broiled by a sizzling summer sun, 51,855 fans sweat it out to see the Eagles, Steve Miller and Eddie Money at Riverfront Stadium's first rock concert. Cincinnati's mayor, Jerry Springer, championed the 1978 concert and allayed other city officials' fears that the fans would harm the stadium and themselves. They didn't. For his efforts, Springer became the concert's master of ceremonies. After the show, he insisted that more rock concerts would be held at the stadium. "We'll do it again. I promise." The city took its time making good on his promise, though. Aside from an annual soul festival, which draws crowds in the tens of thousands and has presented such stars as Luther Vandross, Aretha Franklin and Stevie Wonder, Riverfront did not see another rock concert until the Rolling Stones played there in 1989.

**RIVERFRONT STADIUM'S
FIRST ROCK CONCERT**
August 16, 1978

Dan Dry

Dressed for success, Bootsy Collins smiles behind his "Space Specs" – his nickname for those star-shaped lenses – as a "Get Out the Vote" parade pauses along its route from Winton Hills to the West End.

William "Bootsy" Collins went to Courter Technical High School, played bass guitar in local bands and hung out at King Records' studios in Evanston. His dream, to play for the label's biggest star, James Brown, came true in 1970. At age 16, Collins joined Brown's band and established the thumb-slapping style of funk bass guitar.

King Records was formed in 1944. The label recorded soul, jazz, R&B, blues and country artists, putting 461 records on the charts until King's plant closed in 1970.

Collins later played bass guitar for Parliament-Funkadelic before forming his own group, Bootsy's Rubber Band.

A member of the Rock and Roll Hall of Fame since 1997, Bootsy Collins is one of 11 inductees who recorded for or worked at King. The list includes James Brown, Charles Brown, Jackie Wilson and King's founder, Syd Nathan.

BOOTSY COLLINS
November 3, 1979

Ed Reinke

Hand up, head back, lips together, Max Rudolf hushes his orchestra. The Cincinnati Symphony Orchestra's new music director makes his debut appearance with the ensemble during a Friday afternoon concert at Music Hall. The German-born conductor led the CSO with distinction from 1958 through 1970. With a firm hand and gentle spirit, he saved the orchestra from financial ruin, restored its artistic reputation and brought it international renown. During his tenure, he took the CSO on a world tour in 1966, increased musicians' salaries, set up concerts in schools and parks, and established a series of pops concerts that would evolve into the CSO's perennial money-maker, the Cincinnati Pops Orchestra.

MAX RUDOLF
October 10, 1958

Ran Cochran

NUTCRACKER AUDITION
September 13, 1998

Craig Ruttle

Sunlight setting their tights aglow, six aspiring ballerinas stand in the Cincinnati Ballet's West End rehearsal studio, wondering whether they have passed their auditions.

Tracy Woodburn, Anna Counts, Kelly Whitaker, Kristen Coyle, Tristen Bailey and Sarah Hiance hope to land the role of Clara, central character in *The Nutcracker*. The famed Tchaikovsky work has been the ballet company's holiday production since 1974.

As the six girls wait, they can dream of dancing the ballet as adults. Such dreams came true for the Cincinnati Ballet dancers performing in *The Nutcracker's* "Land of Snow."

Tutus shimmering across Music Hall's stage, the ballerinas turn into snowflakes during a scene from this ballet of timeless enchantment.

CINCINNATI BALLET
MUSIC HALL
December 15, 1994

Michael E. Keating

The day held out the sweet promise of a good time. The Who were in town for a sold-out concert at Riverfront Coliseum. It was a festival-seating show — first-come, first-served.

During the sunny but chilly afternoon, concertgoers gathered on the Coliseum's plaza. As showtime neared, the crowd, thousands strong, surged toward the doors.

Some doors opened. Some didn't.

The crowd pressed forward. People fell. Faces turned blue. The crowd pushed on. Bodies bunched up, some upright like bundles of fence posts, others piled like logs.

Inside, the band played on. Outside, police covered the dead with sheets.

Eleven people lost their lives that night.

Crowd-control rules would change across the nation. Rock concerts would never be the same.

CHAPTER 3

THIS IS THE NEWS

THE WHO CONCERT
RIVERFRONT COLISEUM
December 3, 1979

Ed Reinke

Sounding the call for freedom and brotherhood, Rev. Fred Shuttlesworth resolutely grips a microphone as he speaks from the steps of the Hamilton County Courthouse. Five thousand marchers protesting police brutality in Selma, Alabama stand before him.

As a lieutenant of Rev. Dr. Martin Luther King Jr. and secretary of his Southern Christian Leadership Conference, Rev. Shuttlesworth spent years organizing blacks against Alabama's segregationist policies.

He continued his efforts even after moving to Cincinnati in 1961 to become pastor of Revelation Baptist Church.

Rev. Shuttlesworth knew the tactics of Southern segregationists all too well. In 1956, while he was a pastor in Birmingham, his parsonage was bombed on Christmas night.

**REV. FRED SHUTTLESWORTH
DOWNTOWN**
March 13, 1965

Ran Cochran

Striking his familiar passive pose under arrest, Rev. Maurice McCrackin is hauled to a waiting police car, where he is dumped upside down in the back seat and whisked off to jail — this time for trespassing. Rev. McCrackin and fellow demonstrators had blocked a gate at the Evendale General Electric plant to protest the production of jet engines for Air Force bombers.

Rev. McCrackin was a man of many causes. Over 49 years, he protested war, segregation, military spending, nuclear arms, the death penalty, prison conditions, homelessness and poverty.

By his death at age 92, he had served jail time for, among other violations, not paying income tax and — at age 85 — scaling a fence at the White House.

REV. MAURICE McCRACKIN
EVENDALE
April 17, 1984

Ed Reinke

FREEDOM MARCHERS
UNION TERMINAL
August 27, 1963

Fred Straub

Shafts of light touch the shoulders of passengers in Union Terminal's concourse as they prepare to board the *Washington March Special*. Destination: Union Station, Washington, D.C.

In the nation's capital, they joined 200,000 Americans for the March on Washington.

The march concluded with speeches and songs at the Lincoln Memorial. Bob Dylan sang. So did Peter, Paul & Mary. Jackie Robinson and Josephine Baker spoke.

Before the day was done, Rev. Dr. Martin Luther King Jr. delivered a speech whose words of hope, peace and equality moved to the stirring refrain: "I have a dream . . ."

Standing on the roof of their limousine, President Richard Nixon and Congressman Robert Taft Jr. wave to well-wishers outside the Netherland Hilton. The president was in town for the All-Star Game. Taft – grandson of President William Howard Taft and father of future Ohio Governor Bob Taft – has joined him to stump for votes in Ohio's U.S. Senate race.

Later on, in brand-new Riverfront Stadium, the president threw out the ceremonial first pitches – right-handed, no bounces – to the starting catchers, the Cincinnati Reds' Johnny Bench and the Detroit Tigers' Bill Freehan.

After the players returned the baseballs to the president, he tossed the balls into the stands as the crowd chanted:

"Lay it in there, Dick! Lay it in there, Dick!"

RICHARD M. NIXON
ROBERT TAFT JR.
July 14, 1970

Dick Swaim

72

The day after winning the 1908 presidential election, William Howard Taft takes care of some chores at home.

The only Cincinnatian ever to occupy the White House – and the only person to serve as both president and chief justice of the United States – addresses a hometown crowd at the laying of the cornerstone for a new Woodward High School.

Still standing in Over-the-Rhine, the building now is home to the School for Creative and Performing Arts.

Fatigued from the just-ended campaign to defeat William Jennings Bryan, President-elect Taft, Woodward Class of 1874, tells his audience, "Nothing could induce me to make another speech, after the 400 I have already made, but the sense of obligation that I owe to the Woodward High School for the thoroughness of the education that I received at her hands."

WILLIAM HOWARD TAFT
November 4, 1908

Photographer unknown

Hustler Publisher Larry Flynt is wheeled from the Hamilton County Justice Center after turning himself in to face obscenity charges. The smut peddler has long had a love-hate relationship with Cincinnati. In 1977, a Hamilton County jury found Flynt's *Hustler* magazine obscene. The conviction was overturned on appeal. Still, Flynt wanted another chance to fight an obscenity case in Cincinnati. He got it in 1998. The case ended with a plea bargain that had both sides claiming victory. Flynt's company agreed to plead guilty to two counts of pandering obscenity, and the red-haired hustler promised never again to sell sexually explicit videos in the county. But he was permitted to continue selling his pride and joy, *Hustler* magazine, giving him the last laugh.

LARRY FLYNT
April 30, 1998

Steven M. Herppich

Newport stripper April Flowers (Juanita Hodges) and Tito Carinci, one-time Xavier University star linebacker, are in Newport Police Court for the first of many trials stemming from a botched attempt to frame George Ratterman.

Ratterman, a former Notre Dame and Cleveland Browns quarterback, was a reform candidate for Campbell County sheriff. He had pledged to rid Newport of its reputation as "Sin City" – a center of gambling, prostitution and organized crime.

On May 9, 1961, police arrested Ratterman in Carinci's hotel room. The candidate, drugged with knock-out drops and partially clothed, was in close proximity to Flowers, clad in a fake leopard-skin robe. Carinci was indicted but never convicted; Flowers was not indicted. Charges against Ratterman were dismissed and he was elected sheriff. Newport began to clean up its image.

APRIL FLOWERS, TITO CARINCI
NEWPORT POLICE COURT
May 16, 1961

Ran Cochran

75

Pictures of naked people cause a stir in Cincinnati.

In 1990, the Contemporary Arts Center and its director, Dennis Barrie, were charged with pandering obscenity and illegal use of a child in nudity-related materials after displaying the photography exhibit, *Robert Mapplethorpe: The Perfect Moment.* As jury selection began, protesters marched through downtown in support of the center and the exhibit.

The charges and the trial, which ended in acquittal for Barrie and the center, revived the free-speech debate in Cincinnati and led many to speak out against censorship. Even more people went to see the exhibit, which drew a record-setting attendance of 79,893. An anticipated $110,000 in corporate contributions failed to materialize, but individual CAC memberships increased from 1,675 to 3,348.

MAPPLETHORPE DEMONSTRATION
DOWNTOWN
September 24, 1990

Jim Callaway

Cincinnati police officers respond with Mace
at the 1996 Pepsi Jammin' on Main festival. The
downtown street festival of music, food and fun
was interrupted by concertgoers rioting after
rowdy fans rushed a stage. The show ended with
an unannounced closing act – a chorus line of riot
cops beating out a rhythm with their nightsticks
on see-through shields.

JAMMIN' ON MAIN FESTIVAL
DOWNTOWN
May 12, 1996

Kevin J. Miyazaki

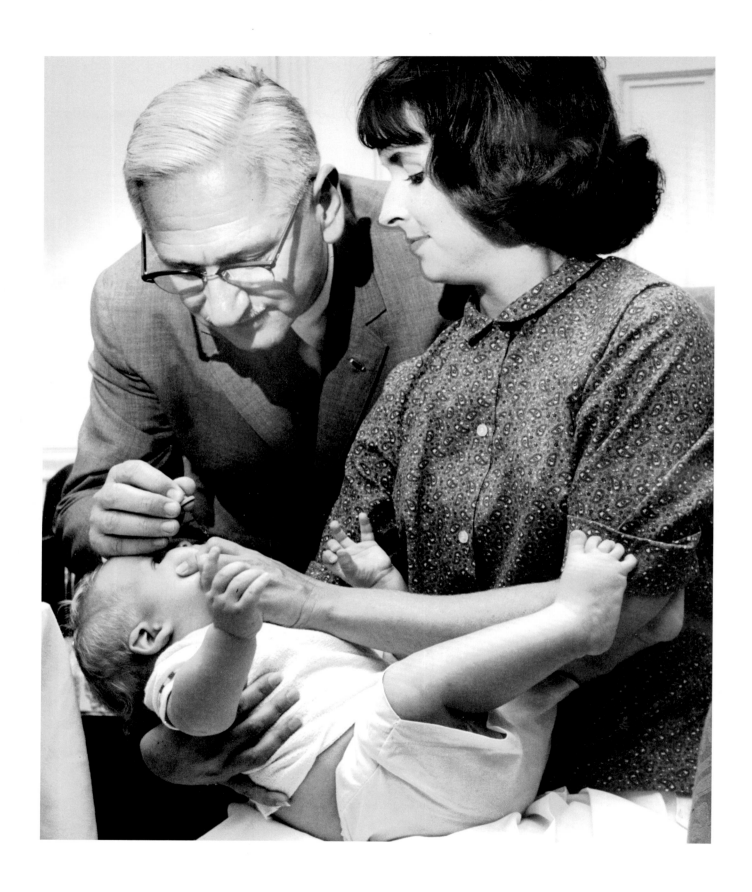

DR. ALBERT B. SABIN
June 23, 1962

Bob Free

Two drops of oral polio vaccine slide down the throat of six-month-old Tom Bross as his mother, Marilyn, gently squeezes his cheeks.

The man guiding the dropper, Dr. Albert B. Sabin, developed the vaccine at Children's Hospital Research Foundation.

The work the Polish native did in Cincinnati would nearly eradicate polio worldwide. Millions were immunized at a series of Sabin Sundays. The first was in Cincinnati on April 24, 1960, but doses were also given throughout the week.

This scene at Stratford Manor Clinic was repeated across the Tristate. Mothers and fathers lined up their boys and girls to receive the free drug — two drops in a teaspoon of cherry syrup — and a lifetime immunity from polio. Dr. Sabin expected 20,000 doses would be given out that first week; 20,000 were administered the first day.

From the time he developed the oral polio vaccine in the late 1950s to his death in 1993, Dr. Sabin insisted the medicine be available at no charge. Although he had every right, he never tried to patent his vaccine. Making money was not his goal. He preferred saving lives.

STRATFORD MANOR CLINIC
MADISONVILLE
April 26, 1960

Bob Free

John F. Kennedy, 35th president of the United States, rides down Fifth Street on a warm Friday afternoon. At his side in the open limousine is Ohio's governor, Michael V. DiSalle.

The president was in Cincinnati to stump for local candidates. He stayed just long enough to give a 10-minute speech from a platform by Fountain Square.

Behind the platform, a woman muttered: "I'm going to shoot the president." As three police officers grabbed her, she hit one in the face with her "weapon" – a camera.

JOHN F. KENNEDY
FIFTH STREET
October 5, 1962

Fred Straub

80

On another warm Friday afternoon,
Cincinnatians again crowd downtown sidewalks,
their attention on President Kennedy. Car doors
swing open. Radios blare. People stand frozen with
disbelief.

The news is bad.

The president had been riding in an open
limousine in another motorcade, in another town,
with another governor. Shots rang out.

The 35th president is dead.

NEWS OF JFK'S ASSASSINATION
SIXTH STREET
November 22, 1963

Ran Cochran

Shotgun at the ready, an officer in riot gear stands at the intersection of Burnet and Northern in Avondale.

On Sunday, June 11, 1967, Avondale was at peace. Rev. Dr. Martin Luther King Jr. visited Zion Baptist Church and told his audience the rallying cry for the summer of 1967 "should not be 'Burn, baby, burn,' but 'Learn, baby, learn.'"

The next night, Avondale was on fire.

Monday's riot was triggered by Sunday's arrest of Peter Frakes at the corner of Rockdale and Reading. Charged with loitering, he had been

carrying a sign protesting the conviction and death sentence of his cousin, Posteal Laskey, whom the press had dubbed the "Cincinnati Strangler."

Word of Frakes' arrest inflamed long-standing tensions in the community. Angry crowds began looting stores, then set them on fire.

The National Guard was called out on June 13 and 750 troops were given orders to shoot to kill. By June 18, the riot was over. Avondale's business district was in ruins, $2.6 million in property had gone up in smoke, and one life had been lost.

AVONDALE RIOT
June 1967

Bob Free

On Good Friday, 1,000 marchers took to the streets of Cincinnati.

This time, they came in peace.

Marking the first anniversary of the death of Rev. Dr. Martin Luther King Jr., a candle-lit procession slowly made its way along downtown streets. Marchers carried signs calling for love, peace, freedom.

One held a poignant reminder: "He had a dream."

**KING REMEMBRANCE
DOWNTOWN**
April 4, 1969

Ran Cochran

Mike Wiseman breaks down at the funeral of his fellow Marine, cousin and best friend, Troy Powell.

Troy was killed in Vietnam. He was one of the 58,000 Americans – 513 from the Tristate – to lose their lives in that controversial war.

Inseparable growing up in Newport, Kentucky, Mike and Troy quit high school together just months shy of graduation. Their plan was to join the Marines and go to Vietnam together.

They also planned to come home together.

Mike returned home in December 1967 to recover from wounds to his legs, back and neck.

Six months later, Troy died when two helicopters collided.

He was 20.

No longer would he send letters home to Mike, closing with the words, "Make love, not war."

**VIETNAM WAR FUNERAL
ALEXANDRIA, KENTUCKY**
May 20, 1969

Tom Hubbard

After a funeral, members of the honor guard from Ralph Fulton VFW Post 6423 in Elsmere, Kentucky salute a fallen soldier. Washing away the lumps in their throats, they gather at Crystal Lake Tavern to share one last beer for a veteran of World War II.

At the grave, the guard folded the flag from the veteran's coffin into a triangle. Each fold precise. Each crease exact.

The flag went to the next of kin with these words: "On behalf of a grateful nation . . . ." Someone played taps. There was a 21-gun salute. A poppy was placed on the coffin. Hands went to foreheads in a sharp salute. The chaplain said: "Farewell, comrade."

**VFW HONOR GUARD
NAPOLEON, KENTUCKY**
October 31, 1996

Kevin J. Miyazaki

The annual memorial service for victims of the Holocaust has just ended. People slowly file out of the Isaac M. Wise Temple.

Holocaust Remembrance Day is over.

Three women who remember the Holocaust every day of the year bare their left forearms. Bela Ouziel stands between her friends, Betty Levine on the left and Carolina Mallah. In the glow of a menorah, they show their tattoos, crudely drawn numbers inked into their skin by Nazi tormentors at a concentration camp called Auschwitz.

These women lived to tell of the horrors in Hitler's death camps, where six million Jews were exterminated. Without speaking, the women deliver a message of courage and survival, a message that declares: Never again.

The time: 6:02 p.m. The weather: hot and humid.

A sweltering summer's day is about to get even warmer. Japan has just surrendered. Church bells ring out the good news. Train whistles howl with delight. Bits of paper rain from office buildings and cover downtown streets. Thousands gather on Fountain Square, stealing kisses, exchanging hugs.

The war is over.

**V-J DAY
FOUNTAIN SQUARE**
August 14, 1945

Robert E. Stigers

Six-year-old Laura Seiffert lifts innocent eyes to receive the flag that draped her father's coffin. Her mother, Janet, stands next to her in the cemetery behind St. Aloysius Gonzaga Church. Laura's three-year-old sister, Heather, clings to her mother.

Laura's father was Robert Seiffert, a Cincinnati police officer. Early one morning, he was gunned down with another officer, Dennis Bennington, during a routine traffic stop. Their killer died in the exchange of gunfire.

Officer Seiffert was 31. Officer Bennington was 27. Cincinnati mourned their passing.

On a December morning 18 years later, another lone gunman killed a pair of Cincinnati officers before turning the gun on himself.

Officer Daniel Pope was 35.

Specialist Ronald Jeter was 34.

Again, the city grieved.

**POLICE FUNERAL
BRIDGETOWN**
March 9, 1979

Mark Treitel

90

Cincinnati Police SWAT team members take target practice with their new .357 Magnums, replacements for the less powerful, traditional police weapon, the .38 Special.

The grimacing officer in the foreground is G. Alan Matthews, later commander of District 3. Next to him is Thomas Streicher Jr. of Price Hill. He became Cincinnati's police chief in 1999, keeping alive a long-standing tradition – since 1912, all of the city's police chiefs have been West Siders.

POLICE TARGET RANGE
INDIAN HILL
March 26, 1980

Dick Swaim

Jerry Springer and Ken Blackwell shake hands at City Hall. At 33, Springer, right, has just been sworn in as mayor – the youngest since Cincinnati adopted the charter form of government in 1924. Blackwell has become vice mayor at age 29.

After 12 years on council, including one year as mayor, Blackwell left city government for federal posts before returning to Ohio.

Appointed Ohio treasurer in 1994, he became the first black to hold a statewide office in Ohio's 191-year history. He later became Ohio's secretary of state.

Springer served on council from 1971 to 1974 and from 1975 to 1981. A sex scandal split his council stints. After news broke that he had been dallying with a prostitute, he resigned in 1974. Re-elected the next year, he served as mayor from 1977 to 1978.

Springer left politics for show biz in 1982, first as a popular local news anchor, then as host of TV's most controversial talk show.

He maintains everything he knows about pitching a fit and tossing a chair, he learned from Cincinnati City Council.

JERRY SPRINGER, KEN BLACKWELL
CITY HALL
December 1, 1977
Gerry Wolter

Theodore M. Berry never hesitated to let
people know what he was thinking. In his strong,
raspy voice, the civil-rights attorney said what he
thought as a member of Cincinnati City Council
in the 1950s, 1960s and 1970s.
  In 1972, he became the city's first black mayor.
  Speaking before protesters who have just
marched into his office on this day, he blasts the
city's police division. Berry likens the police
to oppressive British troops stationed in Boston
before the Revolutionary War.

THEODORE M. BERRY
MAYOR'S OFFICE
May 23, 1975

Ed Reinke

BOBBIE STERNE
COUNCIL CHAMBERS
December 1, 1987

Dick Swaim

After being out of office for two years, Bobbie Sterne was re-elected to Cincinnati's city council in 1987. At her swearing-in ceremony, supporters cheered and held up signs.

"Sterne has returned."

"Woman power is back on council now."

A quiet feminist, the new member of council smiled slightly. Looking embarrassed by all the fuss, she lowered her eyes and gazed at her desk.

Sterne always maintained her dignity.

For 25 years, she was city council's voice of reason in a sea of confusion. Not only did she make good sense, she made history. She became Cincinnati's first elected woman mayor in 1976.

The hallmarks of her style were a quiet demeanor coupled with a fierce sense of caring. Those qualities came in handy early in her life as an Army nurse patching up troops in Europe during World War II.

Bobbie Sterne retired from council in 1998. Her letter of farewell summed up her legacy: "Please, don't forget to put extra money in the budget to slurry and seal-coat the streets; and give special care to the children, the elderly, the sick, the homeless, the poor and the disabled."

MARVIN WARNER
HAMILTON COUNTY COURTHOUSE
April 23, 1991

Gary Landers

Head bowed, Marvin Warner watches a pair of handcuffs encircle his wrists. The financier is about to begin a 42-month prison term for his role in the collapse of his Home State Savings Bank.

Home State failed in 1985. It had pumped hundreds of millions of depositors' funds into a Florida securities firm. When the firm went down, so did Home State. Depositors panicked.

Soon, the panic spread across Ohio to other state-chartered thrifts.

The brother and sister bundled against the cold outside the Northgate branch of Charter Oak Savings had plenty of company. Depositors camped out overnight at savings institutions all over Ohio. They wanted to be first in line to withdraw their money.

After 14 weeks of uncertainty, the crisis was resolved. Until then, thousands of depositors went to bed each night not knowing whether they would ever see their money again.

SAVINGS AND LOAN CRISIS
NORTHGATE
March 17, 1985

Don Denney

Emerging from her fruit cellar, Mary Feldkamp
stands on what's left of her home. Such was the
scene throughout the region after 148 tornadoes
chewed up the Midwest that day. Worst hit was
Xenia, Ohio, where three funnel clouds merged
into one, killing 33 people and turning 2,200
homes and stores into piles of rubble.

DENT
April 3, 1974

Ed Reinke

Family and friends form a circle of prayer with
Wildred and Earl Durham. A pre-dawn tornado
had claimed lives and flattened homes in their
neighborhood.

The storm left an eerie stillness in its wake. No
birds sang. No dogs barked.

One by one, stunned neighbors along Cornell
Road, one of the tornado's many points of
destruction, crawled from shattered houses,
surveyed the damage and counted their blessings.

**TORNADO
MONTGOMERY**
April 9, 1999

Glenn Hartong

The sky turned red the night the Beverly Hills Supper Club burned to the ground. Couples dressed for a night of fun left stunned and covered in ashes as firefighters battled the blaze.

The Southgate, Kentucky club was packed. Grossly overcrowded, some would say later.

The Memorial Day weekend brought in people wearing tuxedos and gowns to enjoy wedding receptions, parties, or dinner plus a show by singer John Davidson.

Fun turned to tragedy as Beverly Hills caught fire and 165 people died. They could not escape the flames, the toxic fumes and the crush of people.

Rescue workers took the dead to a makeshift morgue in the Fort Thomas Armory. On the basketball court's hardwood floor, bodies were put on stretchers and placed in separate rows, for males and for females. Victims' names went from A to Z – Marian Adkins to George Zorick III.

They were executives and homemakers, students and teachers, the nightclub's drummer and his wife.

In the fire's aftermath, building and fire codes changed for the better. No doubt lives were saved.

But those changes came too late for the 165 people who died the night the sky turned red and Beverly Hills burned to the ground.

**BEVERLY HILLS SUPPER CLUB FIRE
SOUTHGATE, KENTUCKY**
May 28, 1977

Gerry Wolter

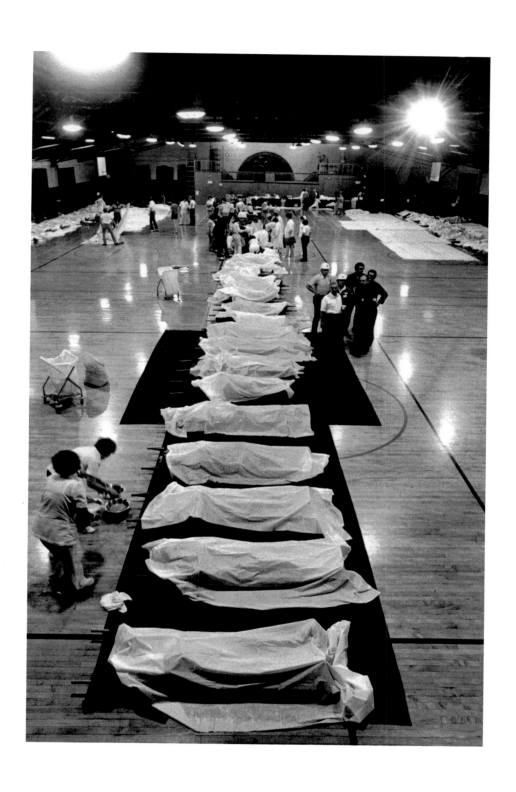

ARMORY
FORT THOMAS, KENTUCKY
May 29, 1977

Ed Reinke

Tears mix with rain and water from fire hoses.

Donna Ayers tries to comfort her friend Robin Ball. But there's no comfort to be found. Lives have been lost, hearts broken.

Fire has hit the white, wood-frame duplex on Tremont Street where Robin lives. Her family's side of the building suffered smoke damage. The other side suffered tragedy.

The Terry family lived there. Flames raced up a flight of stairs and engulfed a second-story bedroom, killing four of Errol and Paula Terry's children: Jason 5, Errol 4, Steve 1 and Silisa 4 weeks.

Yesterday, they were Robin's playmates.

Now they're gone.

FATAL FIRE
FAIRMOUNT
November 9, 1979

Dick Swaim

102

As firefighter Ray Peters emerges from a burning building in Over-the-Rhine, nine-year-old Eric Rembert moves in for a closer look.

"How do you breathe in that?" he asks the masked man.

Cincinnatians have been curious about their firefighters since 1853, when the city established the United States' first professional fire department with a horse-drawn steam engine for pumping water. The city's fire department became the model for the nation. The highly efficient engine replaced hand pumps. And paying firefighters eliminated the battles that broke out when rival volunteer companies arrived at the same fire.

In its first year, Cincinnati's professional fire department cost taxpayers $78,444. By 2000, the tab was $68.4 million.

**FIREFIGHTER
OVER-THE-RHINE**
November 10, 1979

Natalie Fobes

The roof of the Alexander Apartments explodes in a kaleidoscopic fireball. Fanned by 45-mph winds, super-heated air turns the attic into an incinerator. Nearby firefighters recoil from the searing heat of a five-alarm fire. They fear they have just lost some of their own. The firefighters on the roof know other firefighters were inside the four-story building making their way to the attic when the roof blew.

Miraculously, every one of the 115 firefighters on the scene – as well as every person living in the building's 75 apartments – escaped serious injury.

**FIVE-ALARM FIRE
WALNUT HILLS**
April 15, 1993

Glenn Hartong

105

After The Hit and before The Fall,
Peter Edward Rose stands triumphantly at
first base and, by extension, at Baseball's summit.
He has just broken Ty Cobb's record to become
the Major Leagues' all-time hits leader; he basks
in a seven-minute standing ovation before a
Riverfront Stadium crowd of 47,237.

Pete Rose would add 64 more hits to his record.
Then, on August 24, 1989 – nearly four
years after his 4,192nd hit – the Reds' No. 14
would be banned for life from Baseball for betting
on the game he so loved to play.

To many, Pete Rose was more than a
Cincinnati Red. He was Cincinnati. A hometown
boy, he grew up on the West Side and graduated
from Western Hills High School. A hardworking,
selfless team player, he willingly changed positions
to help the Reds win pennants. He ran to
first base when pitchers walked him. Stretching
singles into doubles, and doubles into triples, he
slid head-first into bases, true to his nickname,
"Charlie Hustle," and helped the Reds win World
Championships in 1975 and 1976.

Because of his lifetime ban, Pete Rose cannot
be elected to the Hall of Fame. But even if he
never wins a spot in Cooperstown, he still
occupies a unique niche in baseball history.

CHAPTER 4

CITY OF CHAMPIONS

PETE ROSE
4,192nd HIT, RIVERFRONT STADIUM
September 11, 1985

Michael E. Keating

In Cincinnati, Opening Day at Crosley Field is a religious holiday.

A festive crowd of 28,422 jams the beloved brick-and-concrete stadium, dining on grilled hot dogs slathered with spicy brown mustard.

Organist Ronnie Dale plays "Take Me Out to the Ball Game."

Paul Sommerkamp's baritone voice fills the stadium: *"Now batting, the left fielder, Pete Rose . . . Rose."*

After this game, Crosley Field, site of the Major Leagues' first night game in 1935, saw only three more Opening Days.

In the middle of the 1970 season, the Reds left their home in the gritty West End for brand-new Riverfront Stadium.

But today is Opening Day 1967. It's also a big day for a rookie announcer. Ready to do the fifth-inning play-by-play for his big-league radio debut is former Reds lefthander, Joe Nuxhall.

OPENING DAY
CROSLEY FIELD
April 10, 1967

Herb Heise

108

In an open-ended box of a broadcast booth
nailed to Crosley Field's roof, Waite Hoyt describes
the action.

There's no chance of rain this night. Too bad.
When it rained, Hoyt – Reds announcer from
1942 through 1965 – talked about his days as a
player. He was the ace of the 1927 Yankees.

One hot August night in 1948, before game time,
Hoyt learned his former teammate Babe Ruth had
died. He promised he would talk about Ruth after
the game. He did. Speaking without notes, but
from the heart, he paid tribute to his friend
for two hours.

**WAITE HOYT
CROSLEY FIELD**
June 29, 1954

Herb Heise

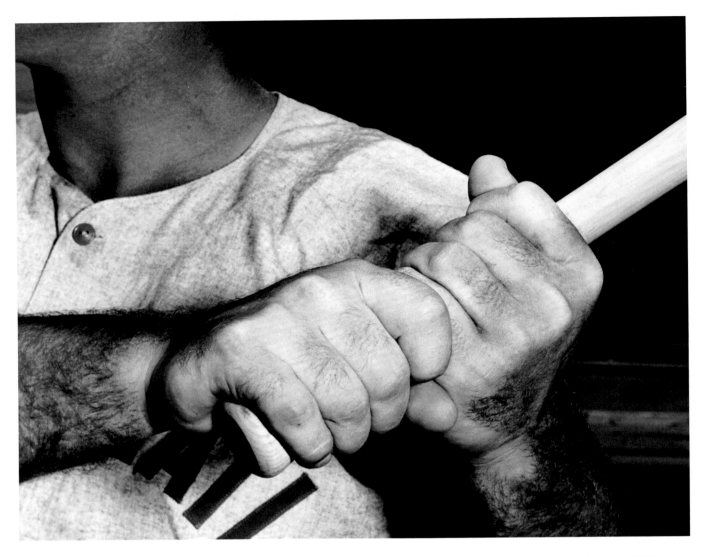

His colossal biceps forced him to cut off his uniform's sleeves. Yet, his heart was even bigger than his arms. When he wasn't hitting home runs, Ted Kluszewski was helping out teammates and perfect strangers alike.

In his prime, 1953-56, no one – not Ted Williams, Mickey Mantle or Willie Mays – hit more big-league home runs than Big Klu. And for five seasons, 1951-1955, he was the National League's best-fielding first baseman.

As batting instructor for the Big Red Machine, Kluszewski kept it simple: Keep your hands up, watch the ball, hit line drives.

Today, Klu's retired No. 18 hangs above Cinergy Field's left-field wall – sleeveless, of course.

TED KLUSZEWSKI
TAMPA, FLORIDA
March 1955

Carl Wellinger

TED KLUSZEWSKI
CROSLEY FIELD
Summer 1956

Allan Kain

From the start, Frank Robinson had all the tools to become National League Rookie of the Year in 1956, Most Valuable Player in 1961.

In 1965, the Reds traded Robinson to Baltimore, claiming he was "an old 30." The aging outfielder won the triple crown in 1966 and was named the American League's MVP.

The Reds retired No. 20 in 1998. A mere 16 years earlier, Robinson had been inducted into the Hall of Fame. He was a young 46.

**FRANK ROBINSON
ROOKIE SEASON
CROSLEY FIELD**
April 1956

Allan Kain

**FRANK ROBINSON
SPRING TRAINING
TAMPA, FLORIDA**
March 1962

Herb Heise

Hot pants and Instamatics greet Johnny Bench as the Reds catcher poses on Camera Day before a game at Riverfront Stadium. The Reds would win the game, drubbing San Diego, 14-1. Bench contributed four hits and two runs batted in.

Fifteen years later, Bench faced another flock of cameras, this time in Cooperstown, New York, for his induction into the Hall of Fame.

The opening lines on his plaque tell his story:

"Redefined standards by which catchers are measured during 17 seasons with 'Big Red Machine.'"

JOHNNY BENCH
RIVERFRONT STADIUM
July 28, 1974

Mark Treitel

They finished first in the National League and they won the World Series. And yet, the 1919 Cincinnati Reds rank as a footnote in history. They beat the infamous "Black Sox," the 1919 Chicago White Sox team involved in throwing the Series. The Reds had a better regular-season record than the White Sox. Cincinnati won 96 games and lost 44. Chicago won 88 and lost 52.

Slim Sallee won 21 games for the Reds.

Hod Eller had 20 victories, plus two in the World Series. Center fielder Edd Roush (top row, third from the right) hit .321 and won the National League batting title.

The Sox had a lifetime .300 hitter in Shoeless Joe Jackson, and a 29-game winner, Eddie Cicotte. Both were in on the fix. Along with six other crooked teammates, they were banned from Baseball for life.

1919 CINCINNATI REDS
Spring 1919

Lawrence J. Neumann

Johnny Vander Meer follows through on a pitch, his left arm flowing across his body. This simple motion tamed his wildness and made him a legend.

Pitching for the 1938 Cincinnati Reds, the 23-year-old tossed back-to-back no-hitters, a feat that has never been duplicated in the Major Leagues.

Vander Meer threw the first no-hitter on June 11, 1938, at Crosley Field. He beat the Boston Braves, 3-0.

Four days later, he no-hit the Brooklyn Dodgers, 6-0, before 38,748 screaming fans packing Ebbets Field for the stadium's first night game. Pitching in front of his parents and 500 fans from his hometown of Midland Park, N.J., Vander Meer stayed out of trouble until the ninth inning. Then he loaded the bases on three straight walks. Vander Meer reminded himself to follow through. For the last out, he coaxed Leo Durocher to loft a soft fly ball to center field. The Reds' Harry Craft caught it, giving Johnny Vander Meer exclusive rights to his new nickname, "Double No-hit."

JOHNNY VANDER MEER
Spring 1939

Robert E. Stigers

114

Tom Browning toasts his perfect game, the first in Reds history and at that time only the 12th in the Major Leagues since 1900.

Striking out seven Los Angeles Dodgers, the left-hander allowed no hits, no runs and no one on base for nine innings.

After Browning struck out the last batter to seal the 1-0 victory, his teammates lifted him to their shoulders before collapsing in a heap of laughter and pats on the back.

"We're all little boys at heart," said third baseman Chris Sabo. "This is what dreams are made of, and he got his dream tonight."

TOM BROWNING'S PERFECT GAME
RIVERFRONT STADIUM
September 16, 1988

Gary Landers

The smiling man with the Coke bottle in his right hand just helped the Reds win the World Series. Jimmie Wilson, 40, started the season as a coach for Reds manager Bill McKechnie (the one being hoisted behind Wilson). After backup catcher Willard Hershberger committed suicide in August and starter Ernie Lombardi sprained an ankle in September, Wilson went behind the plate. He hit .353 during the seven-game series against the Detroit Tigers to help the Reds capture their first – and, so far, only – World Series at home.

1940 WORLD SERIES
CROSLEY FIELD CLUBHOUSE
October 8, 1940

Photographer unknown

The foul pop-up fell out of the sky and into Todd Benzinger's first baseman's mitt. Shortstop Barry Larkin leaped up in celebration.

"And this one belongs to the Reds," as play-by-play man Marty Brennaman said so many times throughout the season.

The Reds' sweep of the Oakland Athletics was a fitting conclusion for the team that had led the National League's West Division from Opening Day to season's end.

The Reds won the final game of the World Series without two star outfielders, Billy Hatcher and Eric Davis, who were injured in the first inning.

The injuries shook the Reds. But they never gave up.

BARRY LARKIN
WORLD SERIES, OAKLAND COLISEUM
October 20, 1990

Michael E. Keating

Admiring his handiwork, Ken Griffey Jr. bids adieu to his 399th career home run, his first as a Red. The next day, the man known to his fans simply as Junior would hit No. 400.

Performing his home-run ritual – a fluid swing, nonchalant toss of the bat and a long gaze – the Moeller High School graduate became the youngest Major Leaguer to reach that plateau. At 30, he already was Player of the Decade and the youngest member of the All-Century Team.

On February 10, 2000, Junior returned to the city where he grew up and the clubhouse where he had regularly visited his dad, Big Red Machine star Ken Griffey Sr. Traded by the Seattle Mariners, Junior signed a nine-year, $116.5 million contract with the Reds, making his homecoming one of the most lucrative – and celebrated – in Cincinnati history.

KEN GRIFFEY JR.
FIRST HOME RUN AS A RED
CINERGY FIELD
April 9, 2000

Craig Ruttle

They are the voices of summer.

First teaming up in 1974 to call Reds' games on radio, Marty Brennaman and Joe Nuxhall have painted pictures with their play-by-play for 27 seasons.

When the home team wins, Marty declares: "And this one belongs to the Reds."

At the end of the broadcast, Joe is "the old left-hander rounding third and heading for home."

Both men are living legends.

On June 10, 1944 – at age 15 – Joe pitched two-thirds of an inning for the Reds, becoming history's youngest big-leaguer. The Hamilton native eventually pitched 16 seasons in the majors, all but one with Cincinnati.

On July 23, 2000, Marty became the 24th announcer inducted into Baseball's Hall of Fame – disproving his long-held assertion that he would always just be known as the guy who followed Al Michaels into the Reds' broadcast booth.

JOE NUXHALL
TAMPA, FLORIDA
April 1953

Photographer unknown

MARTY BRENNAMAN
AND JOE NUXHALL
RIVERFRONT STADIUM
April 10, 1976

Bob Free

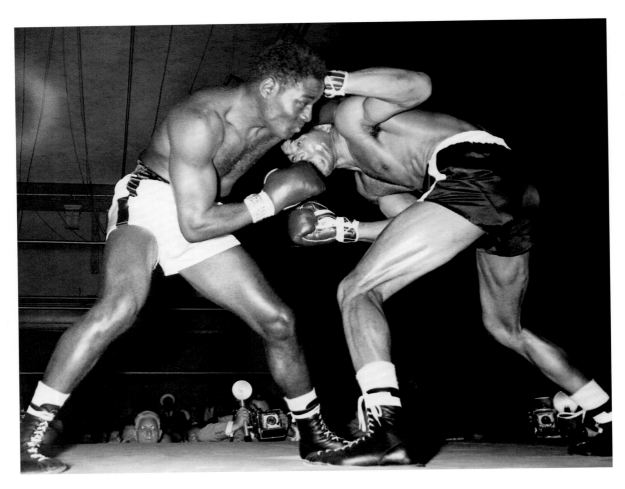

Ezzard Charles gets Johnny Holman's attention with a right to the jaw during a 10-round bout at Music Hall. "The Cincinnati Cobra" won that fight. But later that year, Charles started having trouble avoiding opponents' punches. He thought his timing was off. Instead, it was amyotrophic lateral sclerosis (Lou Gehrig's disease).

Born in Georgia but raised by his grandmother in Cincinnati, Charles became the heavyweight champion of the world on June 22, 1949, when he defeated Jersey Joe Walcott. Charles successfully defended his crown eight times – including a 15-round decision over his idol, Joe Louis, in 1950 – before Walcott knocked him out during a rematch on July 18, 1951.

Named to the Boxing Hall of Fame in 1970, Charles lost his fight with Lou Gehrig's disease in 1975 at age 53.

EZZARD CHARLES
MUSIC HALL
June 8, 1955

Allan Kain

Aaron Pryor takes a victory lap around the crumpled body of
Jose Fernandez. Pryor has made short work of another opponent.
   Pryor's fast fists made him the junior welterweight champion of the world
in 1980. A 39-1 record, with 35 knockouts, earned the Over-the-Rhine
fighter a place in the Boxing Hall of Fame. But wild nights and drugs put
him in the Hall of Shame – eventually robbing him of every penny of the
$5.2 million he had won. By 1999, "The Hawk" was suffering from
pugilistic dementia, the clinical term for "punch drunk," and was having
trouble reliving the victory laps he had once run in the ring.

AARON PRYOR
CINCINNATI GARDENS
June 23, 1979

Michael E. Keating

University of Cincinnati basketball coach Ed Jucker takes a ride atop his players' shoulders. The Bearcats have won the NCAA championship for the second year in a row.

In 1961 and again in 1962, they beat heavily-favored Ohio State to win the NCAA title. In 1963, UC missed a three-peat by three points.

These teams were improbable champs. Oscar Robertson, UC's greatest player, had graduated in 1960. But first-year coach Jucker altered the game plan and groomed his players into what he called his "All-American team."

He transformed UC's star-powered run-and-shoot offense into a deliberate, pick-the-best-shot style, mixed with a high-pressure defense. The Bearcats won with determination, humility and teamwork.

NCAA CHAMPIONSHIP
FREEDOM HALL, LOUISVILLE
March 24, 1962

Bob Free

March Madness strikes. University of Cincinnati basketball coach Bob Huggins goes cheek-to-cheek and loafer-to-sneaker with guard Anthony Buford. This warm and fuzzy moment comes from a coach who prefers to scream when a whisper would work.

The coach and his player were celebrating. UC had beaten Memphis State to advance to the Final Four. (The Bearcats lost to the Michigan Wolverines in the semifinals.)

No UC team had made it this far in college basketball's premier postseason tournament since Ed Jucker's team tried for a three-peat as NCAA champions in 1963.

FINAL FOUR BOUND
KANSAS CITY, MISSOURI
March 29, 1992

Jim Callaway

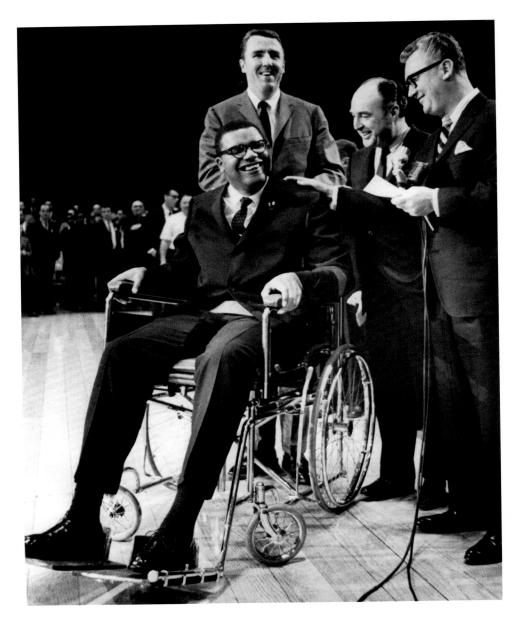

The man strapped in the wheelchair is Maurice Stokes. He once could leap into the air, grab rebounds and shoot baskets so well he was the NBA's rookie of the year. He also made the All-Star team each of his three NBA seasons.

Wheeled onto Cincinnati Gardens' court during halftime ceremonies of the 1966 NBA All-Star Game, Stokes accepts a $1,000 check to help pay his medical expenses. Next to him stand NBA Commissioner J. Walter Kennedy and broadcaster Harry Caray, mike in hand.

The tall man behind Stokes is his former Cincinnati Royals teammate, Jack Twyman. These two men, one black,

one white, defined brotherhood.

After a fall left Stokes incapacitated, Twyman became his legal guardian and made sure his huge hospital bills were paid.

Stokes was 24 when his head hit the floor during a Royals game in 1958. Until his death in 1970, he was partially paralyzed. To communicate, Stokes slowly and painfully tapped out messages on a typewriter. The first went to Twyman.

"How can I ever thank you, Jack?" Stokes asked.

Twyman replied that he had already been thanked enough. He knew a courageous man named Maurice Stokes.

**MAURICE STOKES, JACK TWYMAN
CINCINNATI GARDENS**
January 11, 1966

Herb Heise

Star forward Tyrone Hill takes hold of
The Enquirer's Crosstown trophy. Xavier University
has outgunned the University of Cincinnati,
98-80, in the annual Crosstown Shootout.

The intense rivalry between the two universities
leads to inspired play. UC leads the series, 44-23.
The matchup has featured many titanic struggles
dating to the very first pairing in 1928, when
XU defeated UC, 29-25.

**CROSSTOWN SHOOTOUT
CINCINNATI GARDENS**
January 12, 1988

John Samora

Taking a sweet little jumper inside the lane, Oscar Robertson shoots . . . and scores.

"The Big O" could do it all.

At the University of Cincinnati, Robertson led the nation in scoring. After 14 years in the NBA, including 10 with the Cincinnati Royals, he was inducted into the Hall of Fame.

His 9,887 assists stood as an NBA career record until Magic Johnson broke it in 1991.

Twenty-three years after he retired, Robertson made the most important assist of his life. He donated one of his kidneys to his daughter, Tia.

OSCAR ROBERTSON
CINCINNATI GARDENS
January 13, 1963

Pete Peters

Walking off to chants of *"Who dey! Who dey! Who dey think gonna beat dem Bengals!"* Anthony Munoz leaves the Jungle, the nickname for Riverfront Stadium when the Bengals roared to Super Bowl XXIII.

The all-pro tackle responds with a "We're No. 1" sign. The Bengals have won the AFC Championship, beating the Buffalo Bills, 21-10.

Next stop: Miami and a Super Bowl rematch with the San Francisco 49ers, who had defeated the Bengals in the 1982 title game.

But the Bengals would lose again, 20-16.

Munoz continued to excel at his position until he retired in 1992. Elected to the Pro Football Hall of Fame in 1998 – the first career Bengal to be so honored – he was once again No. 1.

ANTHONY MUNOZ
RIVERFRONT STADIUM
January 8, 1989

John Samora

16th JIM BEAM STAKES
TURFWAY PARK
March 29, 1997

Michael E. Keating

Tragedy rides down the home stretch of the 16th Jim Beam Stakes.

Fighting for the lead in the Kentucky Derby prep race, Inexcessivelygood falls. His legs shoot out from under him and jockey Chris McCarron sails over his shoulder.

Rider and race horse hit the ground. Galloping hooves splatter them with clods of dirt. A passing horse clips the downed jockey.

McCarron received three broken ribs. His horse did not fare as well.

Inexcessivelygood had a broken ankle and had to be destroyed – so close but yet so far from the finish line.

Her brilliant smile earned her the nickname, Pepsodent. Her grit earned her an Olympic gold medal.

At four feet, nine inches, weighing 80 pounds, Amanda Borden was mostly muscle and determination.

The 15-year-old gymnast from Finneytown High School was battling back from a series of ailments and injuries. She overcame them at the 1996 Olympics in Atlanta, winning a gold medal with the U.S. women's gymnastics team. The squad included two other Greater Cincinnatians, coach Mary Lee Tracy and gymnast Jaycie Phelps.

AMANDA BORDEN
CINCINNATI GYMNASTICS ACADEMY
May 21, 1992

Gary Landers

Poised and steely-eyed at 17, Steve Cauthen stands ready to ride for fame and glory.

Both came early to the five-foot, one-inch blacksmith's son from Walton, Kentucky.

Cauthen won his first race as a professional jockey in 1976 at River Downs. Two years later, he won racing's Triple Crown aboard Affirmed.

No other jockey would duplicate that feat for the rest of the 20th century.

Cauthen received high praise from another famous jockey, Eddie Arcaro. Born in Cincinnati and raised in Southgate, Kentucky, Arcaro is the only man to win two Triple Crowns. Of Cauthen, he said: "The only thing that can stop him is the unforeseen."

The unforeseen struck in 1979, when Cauthen went 110 consecutive races without a win.

Cauthen retired from racing in 1993. He was inducted into the National Museum of Racing's Hall of Fame in 1994 after taking 2,794 trips to the winner's circle.

STEVE CAUTHEN
BELMONT PARK
October 6, 1977

Terry Armor

Displaying the form that would win him two Olympic gold medals, Joe Hudepohl plows through the water at the Keating Natatorium.

The Finneytown swimmer set three national records at St. Xavier High School, and expectations were high for the 1992 U.S. Olympics. In Barcelona, he won a gold medal for the 400-meter freestyle relay and a bronze for the 800-meter freestyle relay.

Four years later, the Olympics moved to Atlanta. When the medals for the 800-meter freestyle relay were handed out, Hudepohl joined his teammates to receive the gold.

JOE HUDEPOHL
KEATING NATATORIUM
February 27, 1991

Jim Callaway

Mark Twain saw the game of golf, some folks say, as "a good walk spoiled." He never had a chance to see Jack Nicklaus, Arnold Palmer and Lee Trevino stroll down a fairway together.

The Big Three – winners of 31 major championships from 1958 through 1986 – take their walk down the third fairway of the Jack Nicklaus Sports Center during the opening round of the 1991 Kroger Senior Classic.

The three had never teed off together in tournament play.

The 40,000 spectators on hand knew history was in the making. Traffic to the golf course was backed up for miles. Once on the grounds, much of the crowd lined the links to watch the Big Three play.

None of the legends won the tournament. But all three walked away with the crowd's heart.

JACK NICKLAUS, ARNOLD PALMER, LEE TREVINO
KROGER SENIOR CLASSIC, MASON
July 5, 1991

Ernest Coleman

When baseball was a game and the air was sweet, kids like Richard Boggess of Mount Auburn would choose up sides. Dirt-stained white adhesive tape snaked around chipped bat handles. Frayed shoestrings held gloves together.

"Swing, batter, swing," the catcher chanted.

"Don't hit it to me," outfielders prayed.

They played all day, from right after breakfast until someone called the last player home for supper.

RICHARD BOGGESS
MOUNT AUBURN
March 28, 1960

Ran Cochran

When you're a kid, winning isn't everything.
But goofing off is.
   Hanging upside down like a bunch of monkeys
in the zoo, three Lakota Rockets, Bradley Blyberg,
Ben Lonergan and Ryan Hood, make the most
of their time on the bench.
   Oblivious to the game unfolding in front of
them, the three Little Leaguers work hard at
what should be every kid's full-time job:
having fun.

TRIPLE PLAY
LIBERTY TOWNSHIP
June 4, 1997

Michael Snyder

Heads bowed, shoulder pads lowered, the
Moeller High School Crusaders say one last
Hail Mary with coach Gerry Faust before
crushing Massillon, 30-7.

Moeller is No. 1 again.

The Nippert Stadium victory over the upstate
football powerhouse delivered the fifth state
championship in six years to the program
Faust had created, giving him a record of 174
wins, 17 losses and 2 ties over 18 seasons.

Moeller won the game, but lost its coach.

The day after his 70th victory in the last 71 games,
Faust accepted an offer to coach Notre Dame.

Say one more Hail Mary.

GERRY FAUST
NIPPERT STADIUM
November 23, 1980

Gerry Wolter

Adrenalin rages after a blocked shot.

St. Ursula Academy's Liz Cassinelli (No. 18) roars in victory. Her opponent from Lima Bath High School backs off in defeat.

St. Ursula went on to win Ohio's 1996 Division II state championship — a record-setting fourth consecutive championship for the Bulldogs. No other girls high school volleyball team in Ohio had ever won more than three state titles in a row.

But the Bulldogs weren't finished. Their championship streak, which began in 1993 under coach Julie Perry, reached six in 1998.

ST. URSULA ACADEMY
VOLLEYBALL STATE SEMIFINALS
November 7, 1996

Ernest Coleman

Straining his linebackers' shoulders, a hefty Forrest Gregg hitches a ride to the locker room. The Bengals have defeated the Steelers in Pittsburgh for the AFC Central Division title.

Hall of Fame tackle for Vince Lombardi's Green Bay Packers, Gregg is in his second season coaching the Bengals. The team is going to the playoffs for the first time since 1975, Paul Brown's last year as head coach.

Gregg eventually would lead the Bengals to Super Bowl XVI on January 24, 1982. Linebackers Glenn Cameron and Jim LeClair hoped they would take him for another ride in Pontiac, Michigan's Silverdome. But the Bengals lost to San Francisco, 26-21.

And Gregg walked off the field under his own power.

FORREST GREGG
THREE RIVERS STADIUM, PITTSBURGH
December 13, 1981

Michael E. Keating

Marge Schott stands up to do the wave during the seventh-inning stretch.

That was Marge, owner and fan.

She bought a team that finished last in 1982 and 1983 and supplied a badly needed colorful personality. She paid for the players who won the 1990 World Series.

But she also dismantled the Reds' storied farm system and its scouting department. She offended countless races, creeds and colors with her insensitive remarks. In 1999, after repeated suspensions, she finally was forced by Major League Baseball to sell the team.

In the end, Schott was a tragic figure who came to embody one of her infamous pronouncements about Hitler. She was good in the beginning. But then she went too far.

MARGE SCHOTT
RIVERFRONT STADIUM
May 10, 1985

Ed Reinke

The legend wore a fedora and an overcoat. Five days before receiving the National Football Foundation and Hall of Fame's gold medal for leadership on and off the field, Paul Brown stood once more on the sidelines at Riverfront Stadium.

Padding across the spongy turf, the vice president and general manager of the Cincinnati Bengals admitted it felt good to be on the field again. He had retired from coaching in 1975, after 41 years of championship football teams on the high school, college and professional levels. Even in his retirement, everyone called him "Coach."

Bundled against the chill on that November day, Brown looked ready to take his team downfield one more time for one final victory.

There were plenty of victories in Brown's career. He won 351 games, and lost only 135. He founded two professional football franchises. The Cleveland Browns were named for him. The Bengals brought the National Football League to Cincinnati.

Upon his death in 1991, Brown was remembered for revolutionizing football. He was the first coach to use playbooks, employ assistant coaches year-round and study films of his players in action. The face mask was his invention.

On this afternoon, the coach became one with his trademark hat and coat. The lengthening shadows from the late-in-the-game setting sun transfigured the man into a statue, capturing his profile as well as his status.

PAUL BROWN
RIVERFRONT STADIUM
November 30, 1989

Glenn Hartong

FOREWORD

MVP JOHNNY BENCH
RIVERFRONT STADIUM
August 14, 1970

Bob Free

We were proud to be known as the Big Red Machine. That meant we were powerful.

We won back-to-back World Series and six Most Valuable Player awards. We had Gold Glove winners up the middle, from me to Davey Concepcion at short, Joe Morgan at second and Cesar Geronimo in center. People came early to watch us take batting practice – at home and on the road. Other teams watched, too.

They were impressed by our professionalism, the way we worked together. We truly, truly liked each other. And we were dedicated to one thing – winning.

We had the best individuals at each position, in every role.

Sparky Anderson pushed the buttons and flipped the switches. If you needed a stolen base by Morgan, a run driven in by Tony Perez, you got it.

If you had to have a base hit from Pete Rose to start a rally, you got it.

Davey was as good a shortstop as you'll ever see. We called Cesar "Merlin" because he could hit .300 and catch any ball hit to him.

Also in the outfield we had George Foster, who hit 52 home runs, and Ken Griffey Sr., a .300 hitter who played until he was 41 and could always drop a bunt.

So, when people ask me how good was this ballclub, I just tell them to go down the lineup. We were so good, I don't think we ever doubted we were going to win a ballgame.

All we needed was a chance.

Johnny Bench

142

CHAPTER 5

"AND THIS ONE BELONGS TO THE REDS"

Poised for greatness, members of the Big Red Machine pose atop the team's namesake AstroZamboni. Two days before the playoffs begin, Joe Morgan sits in front, backed by, from left, Ken Griffey, Pete Rose, Don Gullett, Johnny Bench, George Foster, Cesar Geronimo, Dave Concepcion and Tony Perez.

BIG RED MACHINE
RIVERFRONT STADIUM
October 2, 1975

Fred Straub

When an unknown 35-year-old named George "Sparky" Anderson was hired to replace Reds manager Dave Bristol, he was dubbed "Sparky Who?"

Sitting next to Reds general manager Bob Howsam, his co-architect of what would become the Big Red Machine, Anderson knew that 1970 would be a pivotal year for the Reds. On June 24, they would leave tiny Crosley Field, home for 86 seasons and 4,543 games, for spacious new Riverfront Stadium.

Anderson knew how to drive this team. "Sparky Who?" would eventually take the Big Red Machine to four World Series – including the 1970 fall classic – returning home twice as skipper of World Champions.

But Sparky, so-named for his fiery exchanges with umpires, was humble. Minutes after winning the 1970 pennant, he reflected on the managers who had preceded him:

"I'm just a little luckier than the others."

SPARKY ANDERSON, BOB HOWSAM
NETHERLAND HILTON HOTEL
October 9, 1969

Mark Treitel

**JOHNNY BENCH,
SATCH DAVIDSON,
SPARKY ANDERSON
RIVERFRONT STADIUM**
August 27, 1976

Dick Swaim

**FIRST GAME
RIVERFRONT STADIUM**
June 30, 1970

Bob Free

A cloud of dust and a flying batting helmet. Charlie Hustle is safe at home.
Pete Rose's heads-up base-running and .307 batting average led the Reds to the 1972 World Series, which they lost to Oakland in seven games.
Rose's exploits on the base paths gained notoriety at the 1970 All-Star Game. His full-body slam into Cleveland catcher Ray Fosse won the game in the 12th inning – and fractured Fosse's shoulder, ultimately ending his career.
Three seasons later, the 1973 National League MVP tangled with the Mets' Bud Harrelson after a hard slide into second – feet-first this time. Harrelson protested, Rose threw him to the ground, and the benches emptied.
Said Rose later: "I'm no little girl out there."

PETE ROSE, DAVE RADER
RIVERFRONT STADIUM
July 30, 1972

Ed Reinke

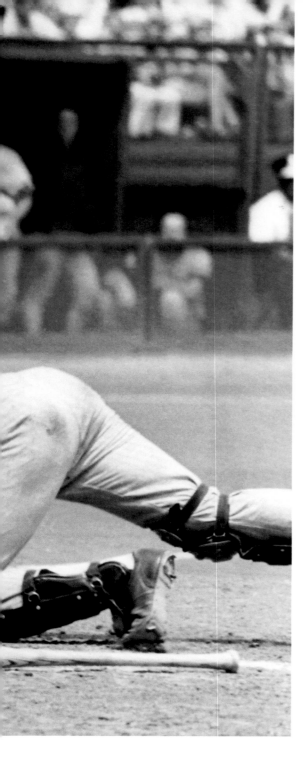

The future looked bright in 1974. Sparky Anderson called his team the "best ever."

The clubhouse was a happy place, with no fewer than three future major-leaguers visiting their dads: Pete Rose Jr., Eduardo Perez and Ken Griffey Jr.

Twenty-six Februarys later, Griffey Jr. would be wearing a Cincinnati uniform with his dad, by then a Reds coach.

The Reds came up short in '74, finishing second in the National League West Division.

But the future was bright indeed.

**THE GRIFFEYS: KEN, KEN JR. (CENTER), CRAIG
REDS CLUBHOUSE, TAMPA, FLORIDA**
February 27, 1974

Fred Straub

147

When the 1975 season opened, third base was wide open.

On May 2, Sparky Anderson asked Pete Rose to move from left field.

Rose didn't like third.

His arm was weak and his fielding inelegant. Still, he switched positions. Anything to help the Reds win.

The transfer opened left field to the power-hitting George Foster.

Two weeks after Rose went to third, the Reds went on a tear, winning 40 of their next 50 games.

Rose eventually perfected a one-bounce throw to nail runners at first, and by the end of the 1976 season had the best fielding percentage of any starting third baseman in the league.

PETE ROSE
THIRD BASE, RIVERFRONT STADIUM
June 10, 1975

Mark Treitel

Morgan to Concepcion to first.
Game over.
The Reds take one from the Phillies.
In the Reds' double-play combinations, Dave Concepcion soared as the man in the middle. Named to nine All-Star teams, Concepcion won five Gold Gloves.
Many of his career statistics top those of famed shortstops Phil Rizzuto and Pee Wee Reese.
Concepcion's numbers came close to the accomplishments of another shortstop, Luis Aparicio – his idol and fellow Venezuelan.
Aparicio, Rizzuto and Reese are in the Hall of Fame. Concepcion still waits to make that leap into baseball immortality.

DAVE CONCEPCION
RIVERFRONT STADIUM
May 25, 1975

Mark Treitel

149

On the eve of Game 3 of the 1975 World Series, the Carew Tower exhorts the home team.

As the Reds stand along the first-base line for "The Star-Spangled Banner," they are tied with the Red Sox, one game apiece.

Game 3 would see a record-tying six home runs (half by the Reds). Still, the matchup would go into extra innings.

In the bottom of the 10th, Reds reserve outfielder Ed Armbrister laid down a bunt. Boston catcher Carlton Fisk charged the ball. Armbrister and Fisk collided. The batter ran to first. The catcher threw the ball away into center field. Despite howls of protest, the umpires ruled no intentional interference.

Three batters later, bases loaded, Joe Morgan drove the fourth pitch deep into center for a single. Cesar Geronimo scored.

Cincinnati 6, Boston 5.

Reds lead, two games to one.

CAREW TOWER
October 13, 1975

Bob Free

GAME 3, 1975 WORLD SERIES
RIVERFRONT STADIUM
October 14, 1975

Fred Straub

See the ball. Hit the ball.

Tony Perez takes his own words to heart. Twice.

He hits two home runs – a solo shot in the fourth inning and a three-run blast in the sixth – to help the Reds win Game 5. The 6-2 victory avenges the 5-4 Boston win the night before that had tied the Series at two games each.

Perez entered the game 0-for-the-Series, hitless in 15 trips to the plate. "You have a chance to set an all-time record," Sparky Anderson needled his first baseman. "Let this go seven games and don't get a hit. Then your children can tell their children that their grandfather had an all-time World Series record – most at-bats without a hit."

Two games later, a third Perez home run would help the Reds win the Series. An even better story to tell his grandchildren.

TONY PEREZ
HOME RUN NO. 1
GAME 5, 1975 WORLD SERIES
RIVERFRONT STADIUM
October 16, 1975

Mark Treitel

TONY PEREZ, PETE ROSE, TED KLUSZEWSKI
HOME RUN NO. 2
GAME 5, 1975 WORLD SERIES
RIVERFRONT STADIUM
October 16, 1975

Bob Free

Don Gullett takes aim, winds up and fires at Johnny Bench's mitt. For 8⅔ innings, Gullett mowed down the Red Sox, holding Boston to two runs on five hits, striking out seven. And issuing but one walk.

At 24, Gullett was the ace of the Reds' staff. The left-hander won 15 games in 1975 and lost just four – despite missing two months with a broken thumb. The '75 Reds had two other 15-game winners: Gary Nolan and Jack Billingham.

The Big Red Machine could boast of only one 20-game winner in its history. (Jim Merritt went 20-12 in 1970.) It wasn't because the starters were weak. It was because of Sparky Anderson's strong faith in his bullpen. He was so quick to pull pitchers in trouble, Dave Concepcion dubbed him Captain Hook.

The Reds won Game 5, 6-2. Gullett got credit for the victory. But not for the complete game.

Summoning top reliever Rawly Eastwick to strike out the final batter, Anderson lifted Gullett with these words: "That's enough for tonight, Donald."

DON GULLETT
GAME 5, 1975 WORLD SERIES
RIVERFRONT STADIUM
October 16, 1975

Fred Straub

Most times when Pete Rose met a catcher, it meant bad news for the man with the shinguards. This time, Carlton Fisk prevailed. The out ended the first inning of Game 5. But the Reds would go on to win, 6-2. And Rose would earn the Series' MVP honors.

For Game 6, play moved to Boston, and the spotlight shifted to Fisk.

In the bottom of the 12th inning, he hit the game-winning home run. Watching the ball arcing toward foul territory, Fisk waved the ball fair with a mighty display of body English. His act would become one of the most replayed images in World Series history.

CARLTON FISK, PETE ROSE
GAME 5, 1975 WORLD SERIES
RIVERFRONT STADIUM
October 16, 1975

Fred Straub

GAME 7, 1975 WORLD SERIES
FENWAY PARK, BOSTON
October 22, 1975

Bob Lynn

Tony Perez gathers Will McEnaney and Pete Rose into his arms. Joe Morgan rushes to join them.

Johnny Bench must be on his way from home plate.

Cesar Geronimo has just caught a soft fly ball hit to center field by Red Sox star Carl Yastrzemski.

Even before the game ended, and an impromptu celebration filled Fountain Square, baseball fans were using superlatives to describe the Series.

"The most dramatic."

"The most memorable."

But one thing should not be overlooked: There was a seventh game in the 1975 World Series.

And the best team won.

**COACH TED KLUSZEWSKI'S
CHAMPIONSHIP RING
RIVERFRONT STADIUM**
April 18, 1976

Bob Free

FOUNTAIN SQUARE
October 22, 1975

Bob Free

A new pennant flies over Riverfront Stadium. Cincinnati has not seen such a precious piece of cloth since the Reds beat the Tigers in the 1940 World Series.

Down on the field, it's business as usual.

A welcoming committee congratulates second-baseman Joe Morgan for driving in Ken Griffey to beat Los Angeles in the ninth inning.

The victory vaulted the Reds over the Dodgers and into first place – a spot the Reds would own for the rest of the year.

CHAMPIONSHIP PENNANT
RIVERFRONT STADIUM
April 18, 1976

Bob Free

The Big Red Machine was a disciplined bunch. Clean-shaven. Hair trimmed. Just the right amount of red on the legs. Suits on the road.

The discipline paid off.

Sparky Anderson's 1976 team won 102 games during the regular season, then swept the playoffs and the World Series.

Pete Rose led the league in hits with 215 and won the Roberto Clemente Award as "a guy who knows how to represent the game on and off the field."

Joe Morgan, Johnny Bench, Cesar Geronimo and Dave Concepcion won Gold Gloves for their unparalleled fielding.

In Game 3 of the Series, Dan Driessen – the National League's first designated hitter – had three hits, including a home run.

No wonder then that after Game 3, some of the team's off-field bosses – Jolene Billingham, Pituka Perez, Karolyn Rose and Carol Nolan – smiled confidently and gave the high sign.

They smelled a sweep.

REDS WIVES
GAME 3, 1976 WORLD SERIES
YANKEE STADIUM
October 19, 1976

Mark Treitel

NATIONAL ANTHEM
GAME 1, 1976 WORLD SERIES
RIVERFRONT STADIUM
October 16, 1976

Mark Treitel

Ninth inning. Reds are down, 6-4.

George Foster launches a 480-foot home run. Johnny Bench follows suit. Game tied.

Four hitters later, the bases are loaded. Ken Griffey singles. Dave Concepcion scores.

The Reds sweep the Phillies. Next stop: World Series.

Good omens rode with Foster's home run. In 1976, the left fielder led the Reds with 29 home runs and the National League with 121 RBI. He would hit .429 in the World Series.

Foster didn't let up. In 1977, his 52 home runs and 149 RBI led the majors – and earned him the league MVP award. His home-run total broke Ted Kluszewski's 1954 club record of 49.

In the 1970s, Big Klu was the Reds' hitting instructor. He found an apt pupil in George Foster.

GEORGE FOSTER
GAME 3, 1976 PLAYOFFS
RIVERFRONT STADIUM
October 12, 1976

Bob Free

Tony Perez congratulates Joe Morgan as he completes
his home-run trot before 54,826 cheering fans. Only
the New York Yankees remain seated.

And it's just the first inning of the 1976 World
Series.

In the Series, Morgan would hit .333 – 13 points
over his average for the '76 season.

And for the second year in a row, the great-fielding,
hard-hitting second baseman with a yen for stealing
bases would be named the National League's Most
Valuable Player.

TONY PEREZ, JOE MORGAN
GAME 1, 1976 WORLD SERIES
RIVERFRONT STADIUM
October 16, 1976

Fred Straub

THURMAN MUNSON, NO. 15
GAME 1, 1976 WORLD SERIES
RIVERFRONT STADIUM
October 16, 1976

Fred Straub

VICTORY CELEBRATION
GAME 3, 1976 PLAYOFFS
RIVERFRONT STADIUM
October 12, 1976

Fred Straub

Ignoring a fan's gibe, catcher Thurman Munson returns to the Yankees' dugout after an unproductive trip to the plate.

The day before, comparing Munson to Reds catcher Johnny Bench, Yankee manager Billy Martin said of No. 15, "I'll take my guy any day."

Munson did have a better season at the plate than Bench. The Yankee catcher hit .302 with 17 home runs and 105 RBI. Bench won the Gold Glove for fielding, but slumped to a .234 average, with 16 home runs and just 74 RBI.

Munson also had a great World Series, hitting .529.

But Bench was better. After hitting .533, with two home runs and six RBI, he was named the Series' MVP.

As the Reds celebrated their 1976 World Series triumph, Sparky Anderson had the last word on the Munson-Bench debate.

"Don't ever compare anybody to Johnny Bench," he said. "Don't never embarrass nobody by comparing them to Johnny Bench."

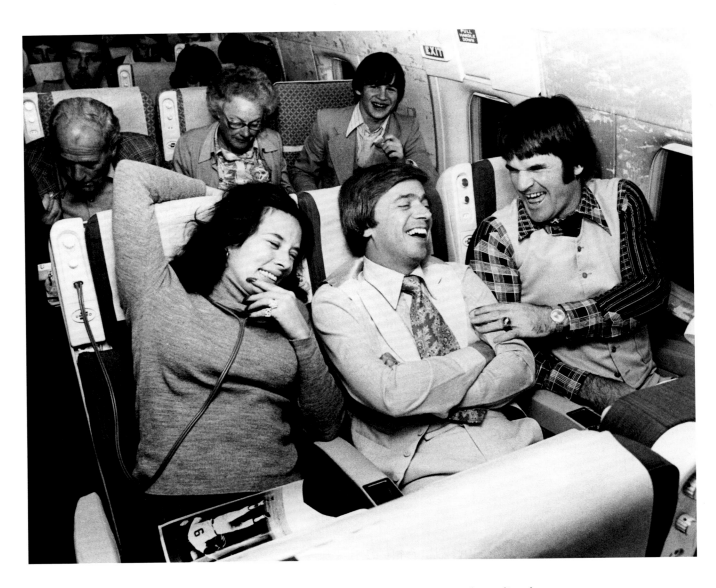

Just hours after the Big Red Machine won its second World Series, Reds radio announcer Marty Brennaman shares a laugh with Pete and Karolyn Rose on the flight home from New York.

The first National League team since the 1921 and 1922 New York Giants to win back-to-back World Series came home to a heroes' welcome. Despite the 39-degree temperature, fans swarmed onto Fountain Square, where the championship trophy glistened in the fall sunlight. Tony Perez chewed on a victory cigar and boomed: "Numero Uno! Numero Uno!"

The good times were short-lived.

The day after the parade, an *Enquirer* article fretted that trades and pending free agency could break up the Big Red Machine. Joe Morgan was quoted saying Reds management planned to get rid of Tony Perez.

"They'll do it to him," Morgan said. "They'll do it to me someday."

Two months to the day after the start of the 1976 World Series, his prediction came true. Perez was traded to Montreal.

It was the beginning of the end for the Big Red Machine.

**KAROLYN ROSE, MARTY BRENNAMAN, PETE ROSE
EN ROUTE TO CINCINNATI**
October 22, 1976

Mark Treitel

Hands up, helmet aloft, Joe Morgan begins his descent to second base. The Mets' Bud Harrelson – Pete Rose's one-time punching bag – waits for the ball.

Too late. Morgan's safe.

The National League MVP has stolen his 320th base as a Red, tying the team's career record set by Bob Bescher in 1913. He would break it three innings later.

Morgan hit with power and ran like the wind. In 1990, his 22 seasons of daring play earned him a place in Baseball's Hall of Fame.

The diminutive second baseman pilfered a total of 689 bases, 406 in a Cincinnati uniform. Morgan remains the team's all-time career base stealer. He left the Reds following the 1979 season to become a free agent.

**JOE MORGAN
REDS' ALL-TIME BASE STEALER
RIVERFRONT STADIUM**
May 21, 1977

Gerry Wolter

Fraternizing with the enemy, Johnny
Bench and Pete Rose enjoy the company of
Tony Perez, friend and former teammate.

Perez drove in his usual 90-plus runs in
1977, adding 78 the next year. But he did
it for the wrong team.

Wronged by Reds officials blind to his
irreplaceable contributions to the Big Red
Machine, Perez became an Expo in 1976
after an off-season trade to Montreal. The
first time he came to bat wearing
Montreal's blue uniform in Cincinnati, a
grinning Perez bantered with Bench.

Banners hung from Riverfront Stadium's
upper decks.

"Welcome back, we love you, Tony."
"Heet a home run."
"We're not the Reds without Perez."

Before Perez could settle into the batter's
box, the cheering fans stood one by one.
Their ovation lasted over a minute. Tony
Perez was never booed in Cincinnati — no
matter what uniform he wore.

The next season, on a chilly May night,
Perez shared a historic moment with Rose.
But it was bittersweet.

By then, the Reds' world had fallen
strangely quiet. The heart and soul of the
Big Red Machine was gone.

JOHNNY BENCH, TONY PEREZ
RIVERFRONT STADIUM
June 10, 1977

Ed Reinke

PETE ROSE, TONY PEREZ
ROSE'S 3,000th HIT
RIVERFRONT STADIUM
May 5, 1978

Fred Straub

168

Eye on the ball, as always, Pete Rose follows the flight path of a third-inning single. His streak continues.

Now at 31 consecutive games, Rose's hitting streak makes the nightly network news. Las Vegas oddsmakers bet Rose won't break Tommy Holmes' modern National League record of 37. The odds are 5-1.

Rose broke Holmes' 33-year-old record on July 25. Joe DiMaggio's 56-game major-league record would prove more elusive.

The streak ended August 1, after Rose tied Wee Willie Keeler's old-time National League mark of 44 straight games set in 1897.

Six days later, Cincinnati moved into first place, and the Reds started to dream of a return trip to the World Series.

But this team would never play another postseason game.

The Big Red Machine's days were numbered.

PETE ROSE
RIVERFRONT STADIUM
July 18, 1978

Tom Hubbard

Alone with his thoughts, Sparky Anderson sees the game, the season and, ultimately, his beloved team slowly slipping through his fingers. The Big Red Machine was breaking down. It would lose that night's game and, in the end, the pennant.

Before the year is out, the dynasty will be history. And Anderson gone.

On November 27, in Room 1118 of the Los Angeles Airport Marriott, Dick Wagner – successor to Reds president and general manager Bob Howsam – fired the team's winningest manager.

Despite unreliable pitching and lingering injuries to Johnny Bench, Joe Morgan and Cesar Geronimo, the Reds ended the 1978 season with 92 wins, good enough to finish second, 2½ games behind the Dodgers.

Wagner fired Anderson in a power play. Always his own man, Anderson refused to be Wagner's yes man. Anderson called the shots – in the dugout and in the clubhouse.

The next season, Anderson signed with Detroit, where he became the first manager to win a World Series in each league. He won so many games with the Tigers, he retired in 1995 trailing only John McGraw and all-time leader Connie Mack in career victories.

In the summer of 2000, Anderson would be inducted into the Hall of Fame. Before making his trip to Cooperstown, he stopped in Cincinnati for a reunion of the Big Red Machine.

The legendary team gathered on the field where its dreams had come true.

All of Anderson's old stars showed up – Bench, Morgan, Perez, Geronimo, Concepcion, Foster, Griffey.

Everyone was there.

Everyone but . . .

SPARKY ANDERSON
RIVERFRONT STADIUM
August 8, 1978

Ed Reinke

Barry Larkin places a lone red rose on third base.

Cinergy Field goes silent.

A murmur begins, then becomes a chant:

"Pete! . . . Pete! . . . PETE!"

Joe Morgan stands at second. Johnny Bench is behind the plate. Tony Perez occupies his old spot at first.

Third base is empty.

Cincinnati's perennial hometown boy cannot come out to take a bow.

Banned from Baseball in 1989, Pete Rose is not allowed to join the Big Red Machine reunion commemorating the 25th anniversary of the 1975 World Series.

Master of ceremonies Marty Brennaman expressed what many were thinking.

"No, we haven't forgotten," he said. "No. 14 should be here and isn't."

From the left-field stands, a fan lowered a "4" next to the replica of Fred Hutchinson's retired number "1," turning the giant shirt of Rose's first big-league manager into a No. 14.

Again, the crowd chanted. "Pete! . . . Pete! . . . Pete!"

Still, the only rose on the field was a flower placed on third as a sign of respect from one homegrown Reds captain to another.

Asked later where the rose came from, Cal Levy, the Reds' marketing director, replied simply:

"God."

BARRY LARKIN
BIG RED MACHINE REUNION
CINERGY FIELD
June 3, 2000

Jeff Swinger

Standing, left to right: Infielder Darrel Chaney, pitcher Jack Billingham, catcher Bill Plummer, pitcher Pedro Borbon, left fielder George Foster (partially obscured), shortstop Dave Concepcion, pitcher Pat Darcy, first baseman Tony Perez, pitcher Will McEnaney, center fielder Cesar Geronimo, infielder Doug Flynn, catcher Johnny Bench, pitcher Fred Norman, pitcher Rawly Eastwick (in rear), bench coach George Scherger. Seated, left to right: Equipment manager Bernie Stowe, third-base coach Alex Grammas, manager Sparky Anderson, president and general manager Bob Howsam, second baseman Joe Morgan, director of player personnel Sheldon "Chief" Bender, pitching coach Larry Shepard. Not pictured (because they were preparing for the night's game as Reds coaches): Right fielder Ken Griffey and pitcher Don Gullett.

They were the Beatles of baseball.
Masters of their craft's fundamentals, the members
of the Big Red Machine played with brilliance and
innovation, dominating their field.

BIG RED MACHINE REUNION
CINERGY FIELD
June 3, 2000

Jeff Swinger

Teammates again among baseball's greatest, Tony
Perez, Hall of Fame 2000, is kissed by a brother-in-
arms, Johnny Bench, Hall of Fame 1989.

"Tony was a brother to me," Bench said later. "He was
the heart and soul of the Big Red Machine.

"Now, he's in the Hall of Fame. It was a long journey.
But he has reached his destination."

TONY PEREZ, JOHNNY BENCH
BASEBALL HALL OF FAME
COOPERSTOWN, NEW YORK
July 23, 2000

Craig Ruttle

Once more, Tony Perez comes through in the clutch.

Returning to his seat after delivering a stirring induction speech, he is congratulated by Marty Brennaman and Sparky Anderson, his friends and fellow Hall of Famers from the Class of 2000.

Nette Stearnes, widow of the Negro Leagues' Norman Thomas "Turkey" Stearnes, looks on. Her late husband, plus one-time Reds nemesis and Boston Red Sox catcher Carlton Fisk were also inducted that day.

But this ceremony belonged to the Reds.

In addition to the three Big Red Machine-era inductees, 19th-century Cincinnati Red John "Bid" McPhee was inducted.

Perez used his speech to talk about respect – how he gave it, how to earn it and why today's ballplayers need to make it their top priority.

Anderson humbly thanked the men he managed. "Players earn this by their skills," he said. "Managers come here, as I did, on their backs."

Brennaman mentioned Reds who should be in the Hall. His list included . . . "Yes, by God, Peter Edward Rose."

Pete Rose was also in Cooperstown. Not to attend the induction ceremonies, but to sign autographs under a tent down the street.

His lifetime ban keeps him on the outside looking in.

**MARTY BRENNAMAN,
SPARKY ANDERSON, TONY PEREZ
BASEBALL HALL OF FAME
COOPERSTOWN, NEW YORK**
July 23, 2000

Craig Ruttle

BIOGRAPHIES

Cliff Radel is a columnist for *The Cincinnati Enquirer.* Since taking that job in 1995, he has been named best columnist by the Cleveland Press Club and the Associated Press of Ohio, as well as the Gannett newspaper chain. In a previous life, he was *The Enquirer's* popular-music critic for 19 seasons. A native West Sider, he has deep Cincinnati roots. His Irish ancestors helped settle Westwood, worked on Union Terminal and joined his hard-headed German ancestors in the area who put in a good day's work and never put on airs. A graduate of the University of Cincinnati, he received a bachelor's degree in psychology, a master's in social psychology and has completed course work for a Ph.D. His work has also appeared in *The New York Times, Chicago Tribune* and *The Washington Post.* He lives on the west side of town with his wife, Debbie.

Sue Lancaster has been *The Enquirer's* news editor since 1996. A native of Bellevue, Washington, she has lived in Greater Cincinnati for 18 years. She holds a bachelor's degree in foreign languages and literatures from Washington State University and master's degrees in German and journalism from The Ohio State University. She also studied at the University of Hamburg, Germany, under a Fulbright fellowship. She has worked as a reporter and editor at several publications and has held a number of editing positions at *The Enquirer,* including deputy sports editor, suburban editor and deputy metro editor. She lives in Delhi Township with her husband, Alan Vonderhaar, *The Enquirer's* auto editor.

Liz Dufour has been the photo director for *The Enquirer* since 1989. A journalism graduate of Arizona State University, she has been a staff photographer for Gannett newspapers in Agana, Guam, Pensacola, Florida, and Cincinnati. Before joining *The Enquirer,* she spent five months traveling around the world for a *USA TODAY* assignment called JetCapade. As photo director at *The Enquirer,* she has coordinated daily photographic coverage in addition to major news events, including the 1990 World Series, 1992 NCAA Final Four, the 1997 Ohio River flood and the 1999 tornado. Over the past 11 years, she has managed the newspaper's transition from film to digital cameras. She and her husband, Jim Callaway, have two children and live in Blue Ash.

CINCINNATI FIXTURES

Christmastime 1968

Allan Kain

ACKNOWLEDGMENTS

The aid, diligence and encouragement of the following people made both editions of *Cincinnati Moments* a reality:

Debbie Radel   Alan Vonderhaar
Ron Huff   Dave Preisser

Also, thanks to *The Enquirer's* Library staff. Ray Zwick, Frank Harmon, Sally Besten, Jeff Suess, Jeremiah Campion and Joe Coffaro always answered our countless requests for one more thing.

In addition, we must thank *The Enquirer's* News copy desk. Cindi Andrews, Dave Bennett, Dick Benson, Gayle Brown, Barrett Brunsman, Jim Calhoun, Dave Herd, Marty Hogan, Nikki Kingery, Jennifer Liu, Beryl Love, Shanna Mooney, Liz Pegram, Pat Tolzmann, Tim VonderBrink and Mark Wert made great catches on these pages.

We are also grateful for the assistance of Cynthia Keller, Laura Chace, Peter Bahra, Linda Bailey and Barb Dawson of the Cincinnati Historical Society, as well as Alice Cornell of the University of Cincinnati Archives and Rare Books Department.

And, many thanks to our bosses. Harry M. Whipple, Ward H. Bushee, Rosemary Goudreau, Pete Johnson, Bill Cieslewicz, Michael Roberts and Rick Green gave us the time, the opportunity and the honor of turning these historic photographs and their stories into *Cincinnati Moments.*

Last, but not least, a special thanks to: Ken Amos, Andy Balterman, Rob Butcher, Jim Callaway, Mick Clay, Randy Cochran, Charles Desmarais, J. Dennis Doherty, John Erardi, Joe Feiertag, Donald Feldkamp, Owen Findsen, Marti Flanagan, Lorene Free, Greg Hand, Blanche Kain, Joe Kay, Michael E. Keating, Cal Levy, Phil Lind, Jim Matthews, Gayle McCaskey, Kitty Morgan, Jack Murray, Greg Noble, Vic Nolting, Karen Phillips, Marian Radel, Mike Ressler, Greg Rhodes, Ed Rider, Ed Rigaud, Mark Roush, Jim Schottelkotte, Dave Sheehy, Gerald T. Silvers, Mike Smith, Ruth Ann Spears, Bernie Stowe, Fred Straub, Cindy Taylor, Diane Wagner and Suzette Winner.

INDEX

AFC Central Division *138*
AFC Championship *127*
Adkins, Marian *100*
Affirmed *131*
Air Force *69*
Alabama *68*
Alexander Apartments *104*
Alexandria, Kentucky *84*
All-American *122*
All-Century Team *118*
All-Star Game (baseball) *72, 146*
All-Star team (baseball) *149*
All-Star team (NBA) *124*
Amberley Village *87*
America *26, 29*
Amyotrophic lateral sclerosis *120*
Ancient Order of Hibernians *34*
Anderson, George "Sparky" *6, 142, 144, 145, 147, 148, 152, 154, 160, 165, 170, 171, 174, 176, 177*
Anderson Ferry *18-19*
Arcaro, Eddie *131*
Aparicio, Luis *149*
Armbrister, Ed *150*
Armistice Day Parade *30-31*
Armor, Terry *131*
Army Day Parade *28-29*
AstroZamboni *143*
Atlanta, Georgia *130, 132*
Auschwitz *86*
Avondale *82*
Ayers, Donna *102*
B&O Railroad *30*
Bailey, Tristen *64, 65*
Baker, Josephine *71*
Ball, Robin *102*
Baltimore Orioles *111*
Banks, The *43*
Barcelona, Spain *132*
Barrie, Dennis *76*
Baseball *106, 113, 173*
Baseball Hall of Fame *106, 111, 112, 119, 149, 167, 171, 176, 177*
Bearcats (University of Cincinnati) *122, 123*
Beatles, The *59, 175*
Beiderbeck, Kay *40*
Belmont Park *131*
Bench, Johnny *6, 72, 112, 142, 143, 145, 154, 157, 160, 162, 164, 165, 168, 171, 173, 174, 175, 176, (back cover)*

Bender, Sheldon "Chief" *174, 175*
Bennett, Tony *50*
Bennington, Dennis *90*
Benzinger, Todd *117*
Berry, Theodore M. *93*
Bescher, Bob *167*
Bethesda Hospital *20*
Beverly Hills Supper Club *100, 101*
Bicentennial Commons *25, 34*
Big Klu *110, 162*
Big O, The *126*
Big Pig Gig *(back cover flap)*
Big Red Machine *4, 6, 110, 112, 118, 142, 143, 144, 154, 160, 166, 168, 169, 171, 173, 174, 175, 176, 177, (back cover)*
Billingham, Jack *154, 174*
Billingham, Jolene *160*
Birmingham, Alabama *68*
"Black Sox" *113*
"Black Sunday" *21*
Blackwell, Ken *92*
Blizzard of '78 *10*
Blyberg, Bradley *135*
Boggess, Richard *134*
Bonanza 12
Boone County, Kentucky *57*
Bootsy's Rubber Band *62*
Borbon, Pedro *174*
Borden, Amanda *130*
Boston, Massachusetts *93, 155, 156*
Boston Braves *114*
Boston Red Sox *150, 152, 154, 157, 177*
Boxing Hall of Fame *120, 121*
Bridgetown *90*
British *93*
Brennaman, Marty *117, 119, 166, 173, 176, 177*
Bristol, Dave *144*
Brooklyn Dodgers *114*
Bross, Marilyn *78, 79*
Bross, Tom *78, 79*
Brown, Charles *62*
Brown, James *62*
Brown, Paul *138, 140-141*
Browning, Tom *115*
Bryan, William Jennings *73*
Buffalo Bills *127*
Buford, Anthony *123*
Bulldogs (St. Ursula) *137*
Burnet Avenue *82*

Burrows, Alex *10*
Bushee, Ward H. *4*
CG&E *48*
"Cadillac" cart *32*
Cairo, Illinois *23*
Callaway, Jim *38, 76, 123, 132*
Camay *56*
Camera Day *112*
Cameron, Glenn *138*
Camp Washington *14-15*
Campbell County, Kentucky *75*
Captain Hook *154*
Caray, Harry *124*
Carew Tower *150*
Carinci, Tito *75*
Cassinelli, Liz *137*
Cauthen, Steve *131*
Celestial Street *50*
Central Parkway *51*
Championship pennant *158*
Chaney, Darrel *174*
Charlie Hustle *106, 146*
Charles, Ezzard *120*
Charter Oak Savings *97*
Cheetahs *184*
Chicago, Illinois *52, (back cover flap)*
Chicago "Black Sox" *113*
Chicago Cubs *52*
Chicago White Sox *113*
Children's Hospital Research Foundation *79*
Christmas *48, 68, 179*
Church of the Immaculate Conception *44*
Cicotte, Eddie *113*
Cincinnati, bicentennial *36*
Cincinnati, mayor of *60, 92, 93, 95*
Cincinnati, vice mayor of *92*
Cincinnati Art Museum *50*
Cincinnati Ballet *64, 65*
Cincinnati Bengals *43, 127, 138, 141*
Cincinnati City Council *92, 93, 94-95*
"Cincinnati Cobra, The" *120*
Cincinnati Enquirer, The 2, 3, 4, 6, 10, 59, 125, 166, (back cover)
Cincinnati Fire Department *103*
Cincinnati Gardens *58, 59, 121, 124, 125, 126*
Cincinnati Gymnastics Academy *130*

Cincinnati/Northern Kentucky International Airport *57*
Cincinnati Police *77, 80, 82, 90, 91, 93*
Cincinnati Police, chief *91*
Cincinnati Pops Orchestra *63*
Cincinnati Reds *4, 6, 8, 32, 43, 52, 72, 106, 108, 109, 111, 112, 113, 114, 115, 116, 117, 118, 119, 139, 142, 143, 144, 146, 147, 148, 149, 150, 152, 154, 155, 158, 160, 162, 165, 166, 167, 168, 169, 171, 173, 177, (back cover)*
Cincinnati riverfront *25, 42*
Cincinnati Royals *124, 126*
"Cincinnati Strangler" *82*
Cincinnati Symphony Orchestra *63*
Cincinnati Zoo *34, 38, 184*
Cinergy Field *43, 110, 118, 172, 173, 174, 175*
City Hall *92*
Civil War *6, 19*
Cleveland Browns *75, 141*
Cleveland Indians *146*
Clifton *50*
Coast Guard *21*
Cobb, Ty *106*
Cochran, Ran *24-25, 63, 68, 75, 81, 83, 134*
Coke *116*
Coleman, Ernest *25, 133, 137*
Collins, William "Bootsy" *62*
Columbia Parkway *44*
Concepcion, Dave *142, 143, 149, 154, 160, 162, 171, 174, (back cover)*
Coney Island *54-55*
Constance, Kentucky *19*
Contemporary Arts Center *76*
Cooperstown, New York *106, 112, 171, 176, 177*
Cornell Road *99*
Counts, Anna *64, 65*
Court Street *31*
Courter Technical High School *62*
Covington, Kentucky *12, 22-23*
Cows on Parade, 1999 *(back cover flap)*
Coyle, Kristen *64, 65*

Craft, Harry *114*
Crisco *56*
Crosley Field *32, 52, 59, 108, 109, 110, 111, 114, 116, 144*
Crosstown Shootout *125*
Crystal Lake Tavern *85*
Dale, Ronnie *108*
Darcy, Pat *174*
Davidson, John *100*
Davidson, Satch *145*
Davidson, Tyler *8*
Davis, Eric *117*
Delta Queen 26-27
Denney, Don *97*
Dent *98*
Designated hitter *160*
Detroit Tigers *72, 116, 158, 171*
DiMaggio, Joe *169*
DiSalle, Michael V. *80*
District 3 *91*
Double no-hit *114*
Drahman, Helen *12*
Driessen, Dan *160*
Driscoll, Jack *30*
Dry, Dan *60-61*
Dufour, Liz *3, 6, 178*
Durham, Earl *99*
Durham, Wildred *99*
Durocher, Leo *114*
Dylan, Bob *71*
Eagles, The *60*
East End *20, 33*
Easter *46-47*
Eastwick, Rawly *154, 174, 175*
Ebbets Field *114*
Eclectic Medical College *20*
Eden Park *16, 17, 46*
Eid al-Fitr *45*
Eller, Hod *113*
Elsmere, Kentucky *85*
Enquirer Building, The *5, 179*
Europe *29, 95*
Evanston *62*
Evendale *69*
Fab Four, The *59*
Fairmount *102*
Fairview *50*
Faust, Gerry *136*
Feast of Breaking Fast *45*
Feldkamp, Mary *98*
Fenway Park *156*
Fernandez, Jose *121*
Fifth Street *5, 34, 48, 80*
50-50 Club 33
Final Four *123*
Finneytown *132*
Finneytown High School *130*
Firefighters *100, 103, 104, 105*
Fires *100, 101, 102, 103, 104, 105*

Fisk, Carlton *150, 155, 177*
Flanagan, Marti *6*
Flood of '37 *4, 5, 20, 21, 22-23*
Flood of '48 *24-25*
Flood of '97 *25*
Florida *97*
Flowers, April *75*
Flynn, Doug *174, 175*
Flynt, Larry *74*
Fobes, Natalie *103*
Fort Thomas, Kentucky *100, 101*
Fort Thomas Armory *100, 101*
Fosse, Ray *146*
Foster, George *142, 143, 148, 162, 171, 174, (back cover)*
Fountain Square *8, 9, 40, 41, 80, 88-89, 157, 166, 179*
Fourth Street *(back cover flap)*
Frakes, Peter *82*
Franklin, Aretha *60*
Free, Bob *57, 58, 59, 78, 79, 82, 119, 122, 142, 145, 150, 153, 157, 158, 162*
Freedom Hall (Louisville, Kentucky) *122*
Freedom Marchers *70-71*
Freehan, Bill *72*
Gamble, James *34, 56*
General Electric *69*
Genius of Water, The *8, 9, 41*
German *40, 63*
Georgia *120*
Geronimo, Cesar *142, 143, 150, 157, 160, 171, 174, 175, (back cover)*
God *173, 177*
Goff, Paul *18, 19*
Gold Glove *142, 149, 160, 165*
Good Friday *44, 83*
Gorilla World *38*
Graeter's *48*
Grammas, Alex *174*
Great American Ball Park *43*
Greater Cincinnati Airport *57*
Green Bay Packers *138*
Gregg, Forrest *138*
Griffey, Craig *147*
Griffey, Ken Jr. *118, 147*
Griffey, Ken Sr. *118, 142, 143, 147, 158, 162, 171, 174, (back cover)*
Guilford School *20*
Gullett, Don *143, 154, 174*
Hail Mary *136*
Hamilton, Ohio *119*
Hamilton County *19, 29, 74*
Hamilton County Courthouse *68, 96*

Hamilton County Justice Center *74*
Harrelson, Bud *146, 167*
Hartong, Glenn *(front cover), 2, 18-19, 36-37, 41, 42-43, 46, 99, 104-105, 140-141*
Hatcher, Billy *117*
Hawk, The *121*
Haynes, Delores *10*
Heise, Herb *9, 46-47, 108, 109, 111, 124*
Herppich, Steven M. *45, 74*
Hershberger, Willard *116*
Hiance, Sarah *64, 65*
Hill, Tyrone *125*
Hitler *29, 86, 139*
Hodges, Juanita *75*
Holman, Johnny *120*
Holmes, Tommy *169*
Holocaust *86, 87*
Holocaust Remembrance Day *86*
Holy Cross-Immaculata Church *44*
Home State Savings Bank *97*
Hood, Ryan *135*
Hostess Cake *22, 23*
Houston Astros *(back cover)*
Howletts Zoo *38*
Howsam, Bob *144, 171, 174*
Hoyt, Waite *109*
Hubbard, Tom *84, 169*
Hudepohl, Joe *132*
Huff, Ron *6*
Huggins, Bob *123*
Hunterman, Lois *20*
Hustler 74
Hutchinson, Fred *173*
Immaculata Church *44*
Inclines *50*
Indian Hill *91*
Inexcessivelygood *129*
Instamatic *112*
Ireland *34*
Irish *34*
Islamic Center of Greater Cincinnati *45*
Island Queen 55
Israel, Yohna *11*
Ivory *56*
Ivorydale *56*
Jack Nicklaus Sports Center *133*
Jackie (gorilla) *38*
Jackson, Shoeless Joe *113*
Japan *89*
Japanese *29*
Jeter, Ronald *90*
Jews *86*
Jim Beam Stakes *128-129*
Johnson, Magic *126*
Jones, Tony *17*
Jucker, Ed *122, 123*
Jungle, The *127*

Junior (Griffey) *118*
Kain, Allan *50, 52-53, 110, 111, 120, 179*
Kansas City, Missouri *123*
Keating, Michael E. *6, 11, 26-27, 65, 107, 117, 121, 128-129, 138, (back cover flap)*
Keating Natatorium *132*
Keeler, Wee Willie *169*
Kennedy, J. Walter *124*
Kennedy, John F. *80, 81*
Kentucky *12, 19, 21, 22-23, 26, 39, 50, 57, 75, 84, 85, 100, 101, 122, 128, 129, 131*
Kentucky Derby *26, 129*
King Records *62*
King Jr., Rev. Martin Luther *68, 71, 82, 83*
Kings Island *55*
Kinsey, Kay *39*
Kluszewski, Ted *110, 153, 157, 162*
Kraft, Annalisa *87*
Kroger Senior Classic *133*
Krohn Conservatory *46-47*
Lakota Rockets *135*
Lancaster, Sue *3, 6, 178*
Landers, Gary *96, 115, 130*
Larkin, Barry *117, 172, 173*
Las Vegas, Nevada *169*
Laskey, Posteal *82*
LeClair, Jim *138*
Lennon, John *59*
Levine, Betty *86, 87*
Levy, Cal *173*
Liberty Street *32*
Liberty Township *135*
Lima Bath High School *137*
Lincoln Memorial *71*
Lindeman, Ruth *30*
Little League *135*
Lombardi, Ernie *116*
Lombardi, Vince *138*
London, England *38*
Lonergan, Ben *135*
Los Angeles, California *171*
Los Angeles Airport Marriott *171*
Los Angeles Dodgers *115, 158, 171*
Lou Gehrig's disease *120*
Louis, Joe *120*
Louisville, Kentucky *21, 26, 122*
Lynn, Bob *12-13, 156*
Lyons, Ruth *33*
Lytle Park *(back cover flap)*
Mabley & Carew *48-49*
Mack, Connie *171*
Madisonville *79*
Mai-Tai (elephant) *34*
Main Street *31*
Majestic 36-37

Major League Baseball *139*
Major Leagues *106, 108, 114, 115, 118, 119, 147, 169, 171*
Mallah, Carolina *86, 87*
Mantle, Mickey *110*
Mapplethorpe, Robert *76*
March Madness *123*
March on Washington *70-71*
Martin, Billy *165*
Mason, Ohio *133*
Massillon (football team) *136*
Matthews, G. Alan *91*
Mays, Willie *110*
McCarron, Chris *129*
McCartney, Paul *59*
McCrackin, Rev. Maurice *69*
McEnaney, Will *157, 174, 175*
McGraw, John *171*
McKechnie, Bill *116*
McPhee, John "Bid" *177*
Memorial Day *100*
Memphis State University *123*
"Merlin" *142*
Merritt, Jim *154*
Miami, Florida *127*
Michaels, Al *119*
Michigan Wolverines *123*
Midland Park, New Jersey *114*
Midwest *98*
Miller, Steve *60*
Miyazaki, Kevin *77, 85*
Moeller High School *118*
Moeller High School Crusaders *136*
Money, Eddie *60*
Montgomery *99*
Montreal Expos *166, 168*
Morgan, Joe *6, 142, 143, 149, 150, 157, 158, 159, 160, 163, 166, 167, 171, 173, 174, (back cover)*
Morton, William N. *31*
Most Valuable Player (1975 World Series) *155*
Most Valuable Player (1976 World Series) *165*
Most Valuable Player (American League) *111*
Most Valuable Player (National League) *111, 142, 146, 162, 163, 167*
Mount Adams *10, 44, 50*
Mount Adams Incline *50*
Mount Auburn *50, 134*
Munoz, Anthony *127*
Munson, Thurman *164, 165*
Music Hall *63, 65, 120*
Muslims *45*
NBA All-Star Game *124*
NBA Hall of Fame *126*
NCAA basketball

championship *122, 123*
Napoleon, Kentucky *85*
Nathan, Syd *62*
National Anthem *150, 161*
National Basketball Association *124, 126*
National Football Foundation and Hall of Fame *141*
National Football League *141*
National Historic Landmark *26*
National League *110, 111, 113, 117, 160, 162, 166, 169*
National League West Division *117, 147*
National Museum of Racing's Hall of Fame *131*
National Register of Historic Places *26*
National Underground Railroad Freedom Center *43*
Nazi *86*
Negro Leagues *177*
Nellans, Dr. Byron *20*
Netherland Hilton *72, 144*
Neumann, Lawrence J. *4, 5, 113*
New Orleans, Louisiana *12*
New York, New York *166*
New York Giants *166*
New York Mets *146, 167*
New York Yankees *109, 163, 165, (back cover)*
Newport, Kentucky *39, 75, 84*
Newport Aquarium *39*
Newport Police Court *75*
Nicklaus, Jack *133*
Nippert Stadium *136*
Nixon, Richard M. *72*
Nolan, Carol *160*
Nolan, Gary *154, (back cover)*
Norman, Fred *174, 175*
Northern Avenue *82*
Northern Kentucky *39*
Northgate *97*
Norwood *30*
Nutcracker, The 64, 65
Nuxhall, Joe *108, 119*
Oakland Athletics *117, 146*
Oakland Coliseum *117*
Oelze, Walter B. *5*
Ohio *12, 23, 72, 80, 92, 97, 98, 133, 137*
Ohio, governor of *72, 80*
Ohio, secretary of state of *92*
Ohio, treasurer of *92*
Ohio National Guard *30, 82*
Ohio River (*front cover*), *2, 7, 8, 12-13, 18-19, 20, 21, 22-23, 24-25, 26-27, 36-37, 39, 43, 50, 55*

Ohio State University *122*
Oktoberfest-Zinzinnati *40*
Olympics *130, 132*
Opening Day *108, 117, (back cover)*
Ouziel, Bela *86, 87*
Over-the-Rhine *32, 73, 103, 121*
Pacific *29*
Palmer, Arnold *133*
Parliament-Funkadelic *62*
Paul Brown Stadium *42-43*
Peanut Jim *32*
Pearl Harbor *29*
Pence, Harry *54-55*
Pepsi Jammin' on Main *77*
Pepsodent *130*
Perez, Eduardo *147*
Perez, Pituka *160*
Perez, Tony *6, 142, 143, 152, 153, 157, 163, 166, 168, 171, 173, 174, 176, 177, (back cover)*
Perfect game *115*
Perry, Julie *137*
Peter, Paul & Mary *71*
Peters, Pete *126*
Peters, Ray *103*
Phelps, Jaycie *130*
Philadelphia Phillies *149, 162*
Pigasus (back cover flap)
Pittsburgh, Pennsylvania *55, 138*
Pittsburgh Steelers *138*
Player of the Decade (Baseball) *118*
Playoffs (1970 Baseball) *144*
Playoffs (1975 Baseball) *143*
Playoffs (1976 Baseball) *160, 162, 164*
Plummer, Bill *174*
Polish *79*
Pontiac, Michigan *138*
Pope, Daniel *90*
Porkopolis (back cover flap)
Powell, Troy *84*
Price Hill *50, 91*
Pro Football Hall of Fame *127, 138*
Probasco, Henry *8*
Procter, William *56*
Procter & Gamble *34, 56*
Pryor, Aaron *121*
Public Landing *36, 55*
Pugilistic dementia *121*
"Queen City of the West" *26, 36*
Radel, Cliff *3, 6-7, 178*
Radel, Debbie *6*
Rader, Dave *146*
Ralph Fulton VFW Post *85*
Ramadan *45*
Ratterman, George *75*
Reading Road *82*

Red Cross *20*
Reddy, Patrick *39*
Reds clubhouse (Tampa) *147*
Reese, Pee Wee *149*
Reinke, Ed *7, 14-15, 40, 62, 67, 69, 93, 98, 101, 139, 146-147, 168, 170, 171*
Rembert, Eric *103*
Revelation Baptist Church *68*
Revolutionary War *93*
River Downs *131*
Riverfront Coliseum *25, 66, 67*
Riverfront Stadium *25, 32, 60-61, 72, 106, 107, 108, 112, 115, 119, 127, 139, 140-141, 142, 143, 144, 145, 146-147, 148, 149, 151, 152, 153, 154, 155, 157, 158, 159, 161, 162, 163, 164, 165, 167, 168, 169, 170, 171, (back cover)*
Rizzuto, Phil *149*
Roberto Clemente Award *160*
Robertson, Oscar *122, 126*
Robertson, Tia *126*
Robinson, Frank *111*
Robinson, Jackie *71*
Rock and Roll Hall of Fame *62*
Rockdale Avenue *82*
Rolling Stones, The *60*
Rookie of the Year (National League) *111*
Rookwood Pottery *50*
Roush, Edd *113*
Rose, Karolyn *160, 166*
Rose, Pete *6, 106, 107, 108, 142, 143, 146, 148, 153, 155, 157, 160, 166, 167, 168, 169, 173, 177, (back cover)*
Rose, Pete Jr. *147*
Rudolf, Max *63*
Ruth, Babe *109*
Ruth Lyons Children's Fund *33*
Ruttle, Craig *39, 64, 118, 176, 177*
Sabin, Dr. Albert B. *78, 79*
Sabin Sundays *79*
Sabo, Chris *115*
St. Aloysius Gonzaga Church *90*
St. Bernard *56*
St. Patrick's Day Parade *34-35*
St. Ursula Academy *137*
St. Xavier High School *132*
Sallee, Slim *113*
Samantha (gorilla) *38*
Samora, John *125, 127*
San Diego Padres *112*

San Francisco, California *50*
San Francisco 49ers *127, 138*
Scherger, George *174, 175*
School for Creative and Performing Arts *73*
Schott, Marge *139*
Seattle Mariners *118*
Seiffert, Heather *90*
Seiffert, Janet *90*
Seiffert, Laura *90*
Seiffert, Robert *90*
Selma, Alabama *68*
Serpentine Wall *25*
Shelton, Peanut Jim *32*
Shepard, Larry *174, 175*
Shillito's *48*
Shuttlesworth, Rev. Fred *68*
Silverdome *138*
"Sin City" *39, 75*
Sixth Street *81*
Snyder, Michael *135*
Sommerkamp, Paul *108*
South Carolina *32*
Southern Christian Leadership Conference *68*
Southgate, Kentucky *100, 131*
Sowmmerfair (back cover flap)
Springer, Jerry *60, 92*
"Star-Spangled Banner, The" *150*
Stearnes, Nette *177*
Stearnes, Norman Thomas "Turkey" *177*
Sterne, Bobbie *94-95*
Steubenville, Ohio *23*
Stigers, Robert E. *28-29, 88-89, 114*
Stokes, Maurice *124*
Stowe, Bernie *174*
Stratford Manor Clinic *79*
Straub, Fred *44, 59, 70-71, 80, 143, 147, 151, 154, 155, 163, 164, 168, 184, (back cover)*
Streetcars *50*
Streicher Jr., Thomas *91*
Subway *51*
Summersell, Justin *41*
Super Bowl XVI *138*

Super Bowl XXIII *127*
Suspension Bridge *(front cover), 2, 22-23, 24-25, 32*
Swaim, Dick *34-35, 72, 91, 94-95, 102, 145, 158-159*
Swinger, Jeff *172, 173, 174-175*
Taft, Bob *72*
Taft, William Howard *72, 73*
Taft Jr., Robert *72*
"Take Me Out to the Ball Game" *108*
Tall Stacks *36-37*
Tampa, Florida *110, 111, 119, 147*
Tchaikovsky *65*
Terry, Errol *102*
Terry, Errol (son) *102*
Terry, Jason *102*
Terry, Paula *102*
Terry, Silisa *102*
Terry, Steve *102*
Thanksgiving *48*
Third Street *21*
Three Rivers Stadium *138*
Tornado *98, 99*
Tracy, Mary Lee *130*
Trains *48, 52-53*
Treitel, Mark *90, 112, 144, 148, 149, 152, 160, 161, 166*
Tremont Street *102*
Trevino, Lee *133*
Triple Crown *131*
Triple crown (Baseball) *111*
Tristate *4, 33, 79, 84*
Truman, Harry *52*
Turfway Park *128-129*
Twain, Mark *133*
"Twist and Shout" *59*
Twyman, Jack *124*
Tyler Davidson Fountain *8, 9, 41, 179*
Typigraphic (back cover flap)
U.S. Congress *31, 72*
U.S. Marines *84*
U.S. Presidents *52, 72, 73, 80, 81*
U.S. Senate *72*
U.S. Supreme Court (Chief

Justice) *73*
U.S. women's gymnastics team *130*
Uncle Tom's Cabin 12
Union Station *71*
Union Terminal *52-53, 70-71*
United States *38, 59, 73, 80, 103, 184*
University of Cincinnati *122, 123, 125, 126*
University of Notre Dame *75, 136*
VFW *85*
V-J Day *88-89*
Vander Meer, Johnny *114*
Vandross, Luther *60*
Venezuela *149*
Veterans Day *31*
Vietnam War *84*
Vine Street *5, 21, 48-49*
Volleyball *137*
Vonderhaar, Alan *6*
Wagner, Dick *171*
Walcott, Jersey Joe *120*
Walnut Hills *105*
Walton, Kentucky *131*
Wareham Drive *10*
Warner, Marvin *96, 97*
Washington, D.C. *71*
Washington March Special 71
Wellinger, Carl *30-31, 33, 48-49, 110*
West Chester *45*
West End *52-53, 62, 65, 108*
West Division (Baseball) *147*
West Side *106*
West Siders *91*
Western Hills High School *106*
Western Hills Viaduct *52*
Whipple, Harry M. *4*
Whitaker, Kelly *64, 65*
White House *69, 73*
Who, The *66, 67*
Williams, Ted *110*
Wilson, Jackie *62*
Wilson, Jimmie *116*
Winton Hills *62*

Wisconsin *30*
Wise, Isaac M. (Temple) *86, 87*
Wiseman, Mike *84*
Wolter, Gerry *32, 92, 100, 136, 167*
Wonder, Stevie *60*
Woodburn, Tracy *64, 65*
Woodward High School *73*
World Champions (Baseball) *4, 6, 106, 144, 157, 158, (back cover)*
World Peace Bell *39*
World Series *8, 116, 142, 144, 152, 155, 169, 171, (back cover)*
World Series (1919) *113*
World Series (1940) *116, 158*
World Series (1970) *144*
World Series (1972) *146*
World Series (1975) *106, 150, 155, 157, 166, 173*
World Series (1975, Game 3) *150, 151*
World Series (1975, Game 5) *152, 153, 154, 155*
World Series (1975, Game 6) *155*
World Series (1975, Game 7) *156, 157*
World Series (1976) *106, 160, 162, 163, 164, 165, 166*
World Series (1976, Game 1) *161, 163, 164, 165*
World Series (1976, Game 3) *160*
World Series (1990) *117, 139*
World War I *31*
World War II *30, 85, 89, 95*
Xavier University *75, 125*
Xenia, Ohio *98*
Yankee Stadium *160, (back cover)*
Yastrzemski, Carl *157*
Zion Baptist Church *82*
Zorick III, George *100*

Poker faces and catty grins radiate from
the first litter of second-generation cheetahs
born in captivity in the United States.

CHEETAH CUBS
CINCINNATI ZOO
August 14, 1978

Fred Straub

184